Jung on Yoga

Insights and Activities
to Awaken
with the Chakras

Dario Nardi, PhD

Thank You

- My mom, Laura Power, for introducing me as a kid to the chakras and their applications, and to my step-dad Richard Power for his youthful adventure stories of shamanism;

- Yehuda Ben Jehoshua and Renato Sampaio for starting me on this journey at midlife; as well as my brother, Chris Nardi, for joining me;

- Nicole Gruel, for pointing me to Jung's talks, found in *The Psychology of Kundalini Yoga*;

- The dedicated shamanic practitioners I've had the joy to benefit from, namely Tatiana Marques, Charles Johnston, Amanda Grover, Bryce Draper, Tricia Eastman, Dr. Joseph Barsuglia, and Layner Mori Huayta;

- Friends on this journey: Libby Schultz and Javier Fernandez, Stephan Beechen and Renee Barnett, Aaron Jonah Young, Dan Stynchula, Jay Dallen, Alex Arndt, Rafael Rios, and Adam Shevel; also, David Litton, for your daily inspirational posts;

- Fellow experts in psychological type, for decades of work: Linda Berens, John Beebe, Peter Geyer, and Steve Myers;

- For editing: Beverly Baroff, Jonathan Bluestein, Nadine Nardi Davidson, Estellaleigh Franenberg, Joe Garand, Sherree Malcolm Godasi, Marisa Reyes, Vicky Jo Varner, and Chris Wood;

- Kundalini teacher and student of Yogi Bhajan, Tej Kaur Khalsa, and the folks at Nine Treasures Yoga in Los Angeles.

© Dario Nardi, August 2017
ISBN: 978-0-9885235-2-4 ; vsn 1.04
Radiance House | PO BOX 691971 Los Angeles, CA 90069, USA
www.RadianceHouse.com
www.JungOnYoga.com

Contents

What's Inside

Consider that 99% of you—this book, your house, your family and pets, and everything else —is empty space. Yes 99%! Atoms are mostly empty space. The material world is barely an outline. Yet here we are, mostly blobs of consciousness interacting with each other, with mysterious origins and purpose. If this is so, then maybe we should get to know this consciousness stuff and work with it.

How's Your Psyche?

We are all wired with the potential to be happy and healthy. Unfortunately, at points in life, we may get caught in a spiral that is unhappy and unhealthy. Consider the following two persons.

Brenda is anxious. Her high-paying tech job is taxing. She's disillusioned with dating. Some days, she wakes unable to stand up straight. She was once confident when presenting her work. Now she hesitates. A long vacation and a return to exercise helped only briefly. Recently, her doctor prescribed medication that makes her feel dull. She feels lonely and powerless and just wants "out." She wonders, what's the rational thing to do?

Gabriel is depressed. His artwork has suffered. When younger, party drugs opened up his creativity. Then, art for the sake of politics was "the answer," but he grew disillusioned. Later, marriage captured his heart but ended "okay." Talking with a therapist has reminded him of his childhood stomach pains and anger at his estranged mother. But he finds talk confusing. Recently, he rediscovered nature and now often hikes alone. Maybe he should move? He often feels inadequate.

Do these stories sound familiar? At times, we all feel disconnected from Nature, each other, our potential, the Divine, or ourselves. Maybe your life is mostly satisfying right now, and you have likely enjoyed a few peak moments in the past. What are you missing? How about the people around you? The sober fact is that we all spend an unfortunate bit of our lives on autopilot, sleep-walking, or on a never-ending treadmill. We hope to get a break, wake up from the bad times, or struggle to stay mindful amid life's distractions.

Now, imagine you discover a treasure. It is not money or an idea. It is a practice. It is for body, heart, mind, and spirit. It is thousands of years old. Whenever you feel out of sorts or caught up in a spiral, you can refer to it. You can try specific exercises and activities. You can reawaken, free yourself, reenergize, get healthier, and prosper again. If such a treasure sounds appealing, this book is for you.

Who's Jung and What's Yoga?

Dr. Carl Gustav Jung (1875—1961) was a famous Swiss psychiatrist who coined many terms we use today such as *archetype*, *introvert*, and *persona*. In the fall of 1932, he gave four lectures* on *kundalini* yoga, an ancient Indian spiritual practice. As a lover of Jung's work as well as a student of this form of yoga, I was delighted to find his lectures on the topic. Those lectures are the basis of this book.

* *C.G. Jung: The Psychology of Kundalini Yoga*, Sonu Shamdasani, Editor. Princeton University Press, 1996.

In the Western world, people are mostly familiar with *hatha* yoga for fitness. It is physical and mental. You stretch and hold poses to develop discipline, flexibility, and mindfulness. *Kundalini* yoga is similar and focuses more on breathing and movement to shift energy and gain insights. It is a constant process of becoming more aware of oneself and others, and then letting go. Kundalini yoga is a fast track to help people activate and work with consciousness. In particular, it works with "chakras," which are psychological energy centers that run along the spine. Dr. Jung focused in depth on these chakras. His insights are the meat of this guide.

Chakra Work is for Everyone!

Anyone can benefit from this book.

Newcomers: If you are unfamiliar with Jung and yoga, I hope to stoke your interest and provide some insight or impetus to start your own journey of awakening.

Fans of Jung: You will learn about yoga in Jung's own words. You will also get a view of consciousness that is based in the body and emotions as well as in the head. This will help you shift from an academic view of the psyche to a more holistic approach.

Psychologists and Neuroscientists: Jung focused on clinical tools from a multicultural view. The chakras are based on people's experiences—physiological and psychological. Think of chakras as a rough guide to tapping the autonomic nervous system and endocrine glands.

Shamans: If you work with medicines like *ayahuasca*, this book is definitely for you. You will recognize many chakra themes from experience. For example, the 2nd chakra links to the storage and release of emotions. This is a resource to integrate your own and others' shamanic experiences.

Yoga Aficionados: Jung's take on kundalini offers a nuanced psychological view of the chakras. Notably, he believed in using symbols, such as chakra *mandalas,* to influence the psyche.

Crafting *Jung on Yoga*

Reading Jung can be challenging. He can throw a dozen ideas into the air and draw out many meanings. I have been a Master Practitioner of Jung's types since 1994. Yet I still struggled with the dense lectures and was ready to throw the book across the room. But I persevered. What he says is profound and differs from his usual topics such as archetypes, dreams, and personality. In many ways, his lectures place a spotlight on the opposite. Kundalini is a means to transcend all of his usual topics. In particular, if you are familiar with his work on psychological types, any resemblance between the chakras and those types is coincidental. That said, Part 4 of this book offers targeted guidance for each type to get the most out of exploring the chakras.

Jung's work, though brilliant, is problematic at points. I had to make editorial choices. Jung visited India but he studied imperfect translations and mostly spoke with other European scholars. These were the primary basis for his talks, which he organized in Austria for the benefit of colleagues and followers. Fortunately, he met an Indian yogi and it appears he privately practiced some yoga. The yogi did not offer kind words for Jung's Western audience at the time. Heeding the feedback, Jung warned that people raised in a Western tradition have different cultural assumptions than Eastern peoples do. He felt Westerners would likely find yoga confusing or even harmful. Ultimately, I had to reconcile Jung's experience of kundalini with the greater body of knowledge about yoga.

As we'll see, Jung's lectures do not precisely align with a typical presentation of the chakras. Historically, over several thousand years, people have presented and utilized the chakras in many ways. For example, the classic seven come with many variants—from three to fifteen or more. There's no one true model or usage. Rather, the chakra system is a therapeutic tool to awaken to greater consciousness. Thus, I have no illusions about locating "truth" here. I offer you a wayfinder to a treasure. This wayfinder is fairly congruent with yoga's historical corpus and Jung's sophisticated approach. You will also find some of today's brain science, which tells us that the elements of consciousness—both as electricity and hormones—work throughout the whole body. I simplify in places and mix in a few contemporary examples. I hope you will be pleased.

Finding Your Way

This booklet is organized into five parts.

Part 1 is an overview. It assumes no prior knowledge of yoga, psychology, or neuroscience. You will also find a detailed step-by-step example of a kundalini exercise that you can try.

Part 2 is the meat. It immerses us in Jung's views of the chakras. I liberally quote him within the six chakras he lectured on. Wherever you see a quote in Part 2, except for the 4th chakra, it is from Jung's 1932 lectures. As is inevitable with Jung, discussions are dense and multi-faceted. Jung's thinking resembles a multi-colored moving spotlight. It keeps granting glimpses of a larger, undefinable organic landscape. To help you, each chakra starts with a snapshot and ends with a set of practical exercises and opportunities for reflection. There are also exercises for yoga, meditation, prayer, and shamanism. These are jumping-off points. Feel free to highlight the text. Draw from your own life experiences. Above all, use this guide while engaging in yoga or similar practices.

Part 3 offers a brief starter course in kundalini yoga. It also touches on *tantra* yoga, which Jung fancied. Afterward, you will find an overview of the nervous system. At the end is a quick guide to the use of entheogens, which are shamanic substances that kick-start awakening.

Part 4 introduces Jung's psychological types and offers advice around those. Many people are familiar with the types or know the Americanized version through Isabel Briggs Myers. This leads into Jung's framework of the psyche and his notion of a Transcendent function. The star here is a detailed chart that offers a fresh, comprehensive view of psychological development.

Part 5 presents a *Wheel of Conscious Experience* as a compass to track your experiences. You will also find four suggested steps to take to make good use of *Jung on Yoga*.

A journey of awakening is always as personal as it is universal. After reading, you may want to get started with your own kundalini practice! I encourage you to visit a local kundalini studio. Or you might get a starter book such as *Introduction to Kundalini Yoga and Meditation* by Guru Rattana. You may find *raja* and *tantra* yoga helpful too. The shamanic practices of indigenous Americans are particularly potent. However you proceed, may your explorations and practices be filled with joyful surprises. May a study of the chakras bring you health, happiness, and holiness.

Part 1

Overview

Kundalini, Chakras, and Jung

As the "yoga of awareness," the purpose of kundalini is to awaken one's Higher Self*. The written teachings of kundalini yoga date back to the fifth century BC in India, and likely longer ago in oral traditions. In the Western world, this yoga only took root in isolated pockets before 1969, when Sihk teacher Yogi Bhajan brought yoga in earnest to the United States. Bhajan wrote, "I am sharing these teachings to create a science of the Total Self…. It is the birthright of every human being to be healthy, happy and holy." He called this "3H."

What is Kundalini Yoga Like?

What do kundalini practices look like? Imagine sitting comfortably, mostly closing your eyes and focusing on your breathing. There are various ways to breathe. You might breathe rapidly and deeply down into the bottom of your lungs as you do gentle exercises. This process oxygenates the blood and soon relaxes you. You forget your cares. This alone is beneficial.

During a typical busy and stressful day, we all tend to get "tightly wound" or we close up to steel ourselves against challenges. We get preoccupied and stiff, mentally and physically, and we may get reactive, close-minded, or hard-hearted. Over time, we may even get accustomed to this contorted state. In contrast, kundalini relaxes, stretches, and opens us. It uncoils us.

Along with breathing, the practice includes stretching, poses, movements, chanting, and maybe visualizing a symbol or scene such as the ocean, a great tree, a holy flame, or gentle clouds. As we try these, we keep refocusing on breathing and the sensations that brings.

With practice, a yoga initiate comes to feel an unmistakable sensation at the base of the spine that pulses its way upward until it reaches the crown of the head, opening the person like a budding flower to an altered state of awareness that diffuses the ego's chatter and defenses.

The Chakras are Energy Centers

As part of its practice, kundalini focuses on *chakras*—psychological energy centers—that run from the bottom of the spine to the crown of the head. The term is pronounced as it is spelled: "chahk-rah" (not "shaka-rah"). The diagram on the opposite page shows the names and locations of the seven major chakras. You will also find a pronunciation guide. You can imagine the chakras as vortices, spinning wheels, or whirlpools that draw us in. Often we can get caught up in a particular chakra, such as getting overly intellectual (all talk) in the 5th chakra. In contrast, kundalini helps us stay flexible and free.

A metaphor for the chakras is the color spectrum. Moving through the chakras is like moving along the colors of the rainbow—from red and orange at one end to blue and purple at the other. Like shifts in color, shifts in consciousness are gradual and yet each chakra has its unique themes, just as different colors matter. Thus, as you read about the chakras in the coming pages, going from the first to last, the themes will shift gradually, and within each are meaningful differences.

* *Introduction to Kundalini Yoga and Meditation: Volume 1* by Guru Rattana. Yoga Technology LLC, 2015.

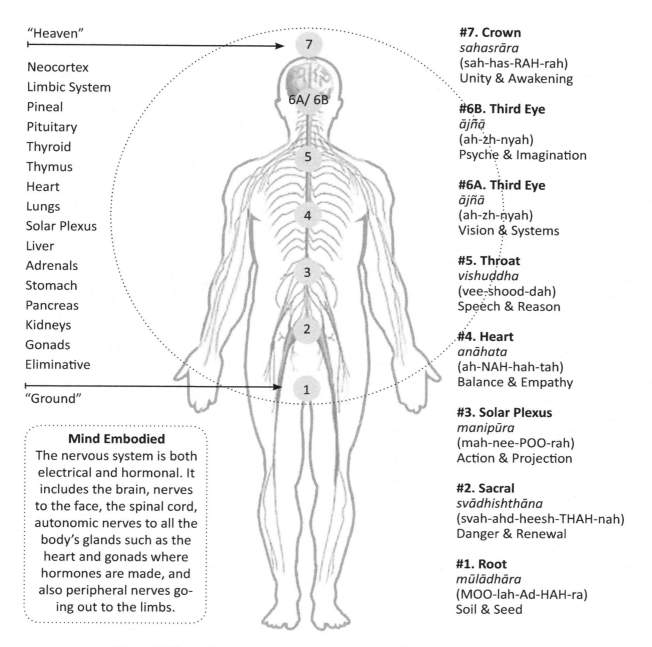

"Heaven"

Neocortex
Limbic System
Pineal
Pituitary
Thyroid
Thymus
Heart
Lungs
Solar Plexus
Liver
Adrenals
Stomach
Pancreas
Kidneys
Gonads
Eliminative

"Ground"

7

6A/ 6B

5

4

3

2

1

#7. Crown
sahasrāra
(sah-has-RAH-rah)
Unity & Awakening

#6B. Third Eye
ājñā
(ah-zh-nyah)
Psyche & Imagination

#6A. Third Eye
ājñā
(ah-zh-nyah)
Vision & Systems

#5. Throat
vishuddha
(vee-shood-dah)
Speech & Reason

#4. Heart
anāhata
(ah-NAH-hah-tah)
Balance & Empathy

#3. Solar Plexus
manipūra
(mah-nee-POO-rah)
Action & Projection

#2. Sacral
svādhishthāna
(svah-ahd-heesh-THAH-nah)
Danger & Renewal

#1. Root
mūlādhāra
(MOO-lah-Ad-HAH-ra)
Soil & Seed

Mind Embodied
The nervous system is both electrical and hormonal. It includes the brain, nerves to the face, the spinal cord, autonomic nerves to all the body's glands such as the heart and gonads where hormones are made, and also peripheral nerves going out to the limbs.

Figure 1: The chakras mirror activity along the entire nervous system

Chakras as Biological Centers

Various traditions describe the chakras in their own ways, but they roughly map to physiological centers in the body*. For example, the sacral chakra usually corresponds to the kidneys and gut—the element of water—and to digestion, cleansing, purging, and so forth in literal and metaphorical senses. In modern medical terms, the chakras likely mirror the activity of the autonomic nervous system, or ANS. The ANS runs throughout the torso, suffusing our organs (heart, lungs, etc.) and endocrine glands (gonads, adrenals, thyroid, etc.). Thus, chakras may correspond to biology.

We can adjust our own bodily activity. For example, we can shift our breathing to alter our heart rate and thus calm or excite ourselves. This can impact the whole ANS. We can hone our awareness of body sensations, such as what parts of us tighten or relax when we focus on certain thoughts. In these ways, we can tune in to our chakras. Kundalini yoga is a systematic way to do this.

With patience, we may further learn to unblock chakras, proactively tap them as resources, and ideally bring them into alignment with each other and one's core self, to live life fully and awake. Thus, chakra work via yoga is a daily practice toward spiritual growth. It differs from prayer but serves the same purpose to nurture a daily link to ourselves, other people, Nature, and the Divine.

Major and Minor Chakras as Vibrational Levels

Most presentations cover seven chakras. Jung covered six in depth. Some who work with chakras cover eight to fifteen chakras, maybe more. Their reason: There are seven major chakras plus five minor ones for twelve total along the body, plus one above and one below the body and one within— as abstract energy centers—for fifteen chakras total. Our palms and soles, plus other points, can also be treated as chakras.

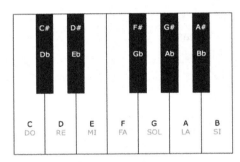

Some people describe the chakras as vibrational levels, like a progression of notes on a piano. You can think of white keys as major chakras, as notes C, D, E, F, G, A, and B. In contrast, black keys are minor chakras. Of course, the notes have a sound such as *Do*, *Re*, and *Mi* for notes C, D, and E. In the same way, kundalini uses traditional sounds, such as *LAM* for the 1st chakra and *OM* for the 7th chakra, to help a person get into experiencing each one.

Chakras as Gateways

Chakras tend to sit between major organs rather than map one-to-one. For example, the 2nd chakra sits between the sex organs and the gut, while the 6th chakra sits between the pituitary and pineal glands. Perhaps each chakra is a midpoint on a path? A path is where energy flows in the nervous system between organs. Thus, the chakra is like a gateway. If the gateway is pinched then energy flows poorly and a person feels discomfort or cut off below that point. A goal, then, of kundalini exercises is to fully open gateways and pump energy along the path. Since our nervous system has two modes—fight-or-flight versus eat-or-sleep—each chakra might really be two gates.

* *The 8 Biotypes* by Laura Power. http://www.biotype.net/types

Your Core Self

Various traditions, including kundalini yoga, describe an extra, all-encompassing chakra that surrounds a person like a bubble. You can see it as the big dotted circle in Figure 1 on page 9. This "aura" is more than a metaphor; it has a biological and psychological basis.

Consider how you have a sense of personal social space. This space determines how close someone can get to you comfortably in casual conversation and such. You also have a perceptual field—sight and sound—within which the brain is quietly alert to dangers; you become aware of disturbances only when something atypical is happening.

You also radiate a purely physical field produced by your heart. This may surprise some people, but it is easily measured even with a smart phone app. The body's systems—namely the heart and brain—generate an electromagnetic (EM) field. The heart's power varies from 1 to 5 millivolts. About 1 meter out, your heart's field will still measure 0.1 to 0.5 millivolts*. A sensitive device can pick up 1/100th that amount, and other peoples' nervous systems can register it unconsciously.

Some yoga masters as well as martial artists train to become aware of and actively direct this core energy by adjusting their breathing, heart rate, focus, and such. More typically, a kundalini student is generally aware of this field and does exercises to feel more harmonious.

Your Turn: *Breath of Fire*

Let's try a common kundalini breathing exercise called *Breath of Fire*. Start by sitting comfortably on the floor with your legs crossed. Sit on a cushion if you like. Close your eyes and mouth and keeping them closed, focus your attention on your nose and navel. You may wish to place a hand on your navel as a reference, at least at the start. Otherwise, rest your hands comfortably on your knees, palms up, with each index finger and thumb touching.

Now, breathe in deeply through your nose until your gut (around your navel) distends. Then let your gut "pop" back into place as you release your breath, emptying your lungs through your nose. Forcefully push out the air, from the navel, drawing your navel toward your spine

Repeat until you find a rhythm, and continue doing this for two minutes. You might use a timer. Ideally, you want to get to one breath per second—quick and forceful. You may need to work up to that goal starting with just thirty rapid, deep breaths. With practice, you can go longer.

During the exercise, you may briefly feel urges to stop. You may even feel slight panic. Assuming you are of at least average health, this feeling is mostly psychological. Your mind is unused to breathing this way. If you feel this urge, just note it and continue breathing, slowing down if needed, then speeding up again when you can. You will be fine.

When you finish, assuming you worked up to a good speed, you will likely feel a rush, tingling, or pulsing in your head. You can focus on this feeling to enhance it. Also, your inner voice will likely be quiet for a time. Just sit and enjoy the sensation, perhaps noticing when your mind starts to get active again, and what that feels like. Or, pose a question to yourself and explore whatever comes up.

* Field Intensity = Power divided by 4 times 3.14 * the distance squared

Kundalini Impacts the Body and Brain

We can measure the impact of kundalini yoga. Neuroscientists have monitored heart rate, brain activity, and such while people meditate. During a simple generic meditation to clear the mind and relax, heart rate and brain activity also relax. Moreover, people who are experienced meditators see greater reductions than those without experience.

People who practice kundalini yoga tend to enjoy extra benefits because they focus on moving energy. After just a few weeks of daily practice, they can show a brainwave pattern normally associated with a strong body connection. More than an empty mind, they show strong mind-body awareness. Body-mind awareness is important to notice and release stress, identify our emotions, and alter habitual behavior. Movement in kundalini helps change our actions as well as thinking and feelings.

During kundalini, when energy reaches the crown of the head, what happens? Is it special? Yes it is!* I asked a friend to help me find out. I used an EEG machine to observe his brain activity. Within a few minutes, he got into a strange trance-like state. From the outside, he was unresponsive. However, his brain activity said otherwise. His brain was active yet also even, like synchronized dancers.

A chaotic brain... 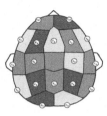 or a rigid brain... 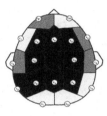 becomes a zen brain.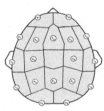

What was happening? His brain regions were in synch, working as one. Importantly, a brain network associated with the ego was quiet. Also, brainwaves associated with body connection and high-level learning dominated. Other brainwaves linked to habitual activity and reward-and-punishment behavior were suppressed. This was not his normal baseline brain. Nor did it look like creative flow or simple meditation. When he "woke up," he was relaxed yet also talkative as he recounted lessons he had gleaned. He was unusually peaceful and joyous for quite a while after.

With practice, people learn to carry kundalini's benefits into everyday life. As part of this, their scope of consciousness, psychology, and behavior also start to shift. How is this possible?

Yoga works because the body and mind link together. Rather than go into all the details now, here is an example. Imagine, when you spot an attractive face, your visual system gets active to process that face a little differently than other faces. Older and newer brain regions activate. Consciously, you may focus on the person's words or such. Unconsciously your ancient animal brain stays hooked for more primal reasons that arouse you. Signals go down through your whole nervous system to your organs. Your heart quickens and your stomach flutters. Moreover, when you daydream later, you can visualize that attractive person again in your mind's eye to get much of the same effect. Thus, both experience and imagination are powerful. Because yoga exercises tap both of these, yoga is powerful too. Part 3 explores the science of yoga in more detail.

* *Your Brain in Altered States* [PDF PowerPoint] by Dario Nardi. http://www.Facebook.com/NeuroTypes

Enter Dr. Jung

Dr. Carl Gustav Jung (1875—1961) was a Swiss psychiatrist. Over his lifetime, he made many contributions to psychology and other disciplines, including anthropology and religious studies. He elaborated on many concepts you may have heard. There are archetypes, the collective unconscious, complexes, the persona, and the shadow, to name a few. In addition to a private practice, he visited and studied many cultures in search of universal themes and processes. From all that, he offered deep insights into human development. His insights continue to resonate with many people today.

Of interest here, in the Fall of 1932 he gave four lectures on kundalini yoga. Likely, he also practiced some yoga for himself. That was highly unusual in his era. His insights are particularly relevant because of his sophisticated approach that places kundalini within a broad cross-cultural context.

Jung Explored the Chakras

What did Dr. Carl Jung say? His lectures focused mainly on the chakras. He had a lot to say about their impact on a person's consciousness and psychology. He delved into the history, mythology, sociology, physiology, and of course psychology of the chakras. For example, as you will find out, he described how each chakra comes with a seal—an integrated set of symbols. He explained how each symbol acts as a learning aid to deduce and recall that chakra's meaning. He illustrated their Hindu meanings with Biblical examples, many of which you will find in the coming pages. Jung also described how other cultures have located consciousness within different areas of the body other than the head, such as locating the self in the heart or diaphragm. Chakra work can even evoke *numinous* (spiritual) experiences. Mostly, Jung focused on the psychology of the chakras, which I will focus on here too.

Chakras are Resources and Spiritual Levels

Historically, there are two basic approaches to work with chakras. One approach treats the chakras as resource centers. The other approach treats the chakras as levels of consciousness.

In the first approach, chakras are resource centers. Each center has a theme that generally corresponds to its place in the body, such as *love* in the heart chakra or *communication* in the throat chakra. For each person, chakras are more or less functional and express in personal ways. Chakra-based practices can help us better tap these resources and we can work on them in any order. This approach is accessible to most people and is typical of many current yoga practices.

In the second approach, chakras are levels of consciousness. Each level builds upon the others. Ideally, when we engage in practices like kundalini yoga, we start with the basics at ground level and move upward, progressively awakening, facing and processing each chakra's themes. This approach finds most people in lower chakras, a minority in middle chakras, and very few in synch with higher chakras. Jung focused on this second approach*.

Both of these approaches have value and neither is "truer." Consider what we know from physics: light travels both as a particle and a wave. Both descriptions of light are valid and complement each other. In the same way, you can keep both approaches in mind as you work with the chakras.

* "Carl Jung and the Kundalini" by John Henshaw in *Knowledge of Reality*, Issue 12-2, 2006.

We Move Through the Chakras

Over the course of a day, we all move in and out of the chakras. As Jung says, "We begin in the head; we identify with our eyes and our consciousness: quite detached and objective, we survey the world. That is *ājñā*." We may also use our imagination to interpret what we see. And as a practical matter, since we "cannot linger forever in the pure spheres of detached observation, we must bring our thoughts into reality." So, "we voice them and so trust them to the air. When we clothe our knowledge in words, we are in the region of *vishuddha*, or the throat center. But as soon as we say something that is especially difficult, or that causes us positive or negative feelings, we have a throbbing of the heart, and then the *anāhata* center begins to be activated. And still another step further, when for example a dispute with someone starts up, when we have become irritable and angry and get beside ourselves, then we are in *manipūra*." If this dispute is highly impactful, it may even stick with us deep down in our gut, in the *svādhishthāna* chakra.

In this example, we started at the top, from a place of calm awareness, and dropped down into "lower levels" of consciousness, where we are less detached and more enmeshed in a situation. We can also take the opposite view—that life is mostly dull as we walk through our days asleep in our lowest chakra, *mūlādhāra*. Then sometimes we get roaring drunk or do yoga, find religion or fall in love, and we ascend briefly to higher chakras. Thus there are many ways to apply the chakras as a guide to understanding shifts in consciousness.

From Material to Spiritual Experience

Spiritual teacher Ram Dass also describes how we move through the chakras. He asks us to imagine noticing someone on the street. We might simply notice the person's physical attributes and actions, such as height and direction of walking, without carefully analyzing. We attend to what's on the outside. That is the material perspective of the 1st chakra. Then we can analyze: What does the person's facial expressions, clothing style, gait, and so forth suggest about his or her situation? And do we find them attractive? This is how we often interact with people as we get to know them on a day-to-day basis. That's the 2nd chakra. Next, we can project onto people some mythic qualities: heroism or villainy. Maybe we learn that a person's ideology differs from our own, and we get oppositional with him. Or maybe we see a person rescue a child and treat her as a hero. Whatever the details, we start projecting all sorts of things, as if we were interacting in a dramatic stageplay. Even if we uplift others as paragons, we dehumanize them, and our projecting says more about us than them. That's the 3rd chakra. Ram Dass concludes his example with the 4th chakra. He describes two people in spacesuits. The suits are just costumes. Inside, we notice each other as conscious souls, and we say, "Hi there!" This is a deep authentic place where we treat others as spiritual beings who are having a human experience.

Consciousness, Ego, and Baggage

Jung links the chakras to stages of spiritual awakening or levels of consciousness, so we might want to know what consciousness is. Scientists lack agreement on an answer. But we all know how it feels to gain or lose consciousness, such as when we wake in the morning. We can be half-conscious, too, or have impaired consciousness from alcohol or drugs, or act mindlessly, such as while driving to a familiar place. In short, consciousness isn't one thing. There are gradations and facets.

Jung observed that a major facet of our psyche is the *ego*. Ego seeks to sustain a coherent sense of oneself in the world. It bridges our inner and outer worlds as a "central command center" and is responsible for reality testing and a sense of personal identity. To do its job, the ego forms goals, set boundaries, and deploys defenses. In neuroscience, the ego likely maps to our brain's executive centers in the prefrontal cortex and to the *default network*, a brain loop that helps to direct our attention, drive our inner monologue, and maintain our sense of self. Moreover, the ego is highly resilient, adapting to whatever might subvert our established sense of self. Jung proposes that our ego may be the "only truly solid piece of ourselves" that we possess! The table below puts the ego in context.

	More Private (Self)	More Public (Society)
More Conscious	**Ego** = "I" or "me." Your heroic sense of self. Feels self-defined. Maintains itself.	**Persona** = Masks you wear. Acceptable behaviors and appearances for others.
More Unconscious	**Shadow** = Rejected parts that may bring you distress or you project onto others.	**Archetypes** = Universal images, roles, and themes rooted in biology and history.

In kundalini, everything in the table above is a masquerade. For example, we may easily confuse the ego for our *only* real self and mistake its biases, games, scripted lines, and props as the ultimate reality. It is perfectly fun and often fruitful to take on an identity like a stage actor, but we may forget we are playing and get lost in a role, like children playing house or playing war. Fortunately, kundalini helps us take off masks, drop baggage, and soften the boundaries between ego and other aspects of ourselves. This "soften and clear" process may feel confusing or hard, particularly when we feel invested, hurt or afraid. Thus, the ego tends to resist practices such as yoga that quiet it and reawaken us. Fortunately, we have choices. Consider the baggage below. Where might you want to lighten your load?

assumptions when you exist	hurts/fears when you feel	projections when you struggle	defenses when you love	excuses when you speak	filters when you see	masks when you imagine

Beyond ego and baggage, chakra work addresses many facets of consciousness, such as being self-conscious, exerting willpower, and listening to one's conscience. Jung used the chakras as a framework to better understand how we develop. He also viewed the chakras as a therapeutic tool that goes beyond talk and analysis to get in touch with the whole person, which includes the body. The table on the next page offers a summary of the chakras with facets of consciousness.

Table 1: Chakras as Resource Centers

No.	Name & Element	Themes	Unfolding of Consciousness
7	**Crown** *sahasrāra* Light	Unity & Awakening	You cultivate the Divine. You shed all masks and baggage, the ego vanishes, and "you" enjoy fully unimpeded pure consciousness, linking to the Divine and granting spiritual detachment, insight, and compassion. Can be fleeting.
6B	**Third Eye** *ājñā* Ether	Psyche & Imagination	You cultivate creativity. You create your own meanings and identities as you consciously play with the many ways you might be. You transform life using symbols, narratives, and archetypes. Can be disorienting, insightful, or manipulative.
6A	**Third Eye** *ājñā* Metal*	Vision & Systems	You cultivate integrity. You build your ego to be more sophisticated and productive toward a vision. You align with the world as it actually is. Can be virtuous, prideful, or tyrannical.
5	**Throat** *vishuddha* Air	Speech & Reason	You cultivate fluency. You consciously observe, assess, and question your ego and your own and others' behavior. You strive for objective, scientific self-development to remove your own biases. You can be critical, verbose, or impersonal.
4	**Heart** *anāhata* Wood*	Balance & Empathy	You cultivate love. You follow your inner guide as you commit to moderating activities and cooperative relationships so as to grow with others. You gravitate toward those who complement your gifts and offset your pitfalls.
3	**Solar Plexus** *manipūra* Fire	Action & Projection	You cultivate power. You consciously embrace and sell your strengths. You draw on willpower, clarify your purpose, and celebrate truth. You idealize, ignore, or vilify what differs from you. This can be empowering or extreme with a cause.
2	**Sacral** *svādhishthāna* Water	Danger & Renewal	You cultivate fulfillment. You seek ways to meet your needs, socialize, find extra pleasures, procreate, dump baggage, and deal with life's conflicts and options. Can be self-conscious.
1	**Root** *mūlādhāra* Earth	Soil & Seed	You cultivate survival. You are aware of the environment, follow cultural norms, and focus on meeting basic material needs by eating, sleeping, and such. Can be harsh or dull.

* These are atypical assignments. See the chakra descriptions in Part 2 for details.

Daily Life in the Chakras

We can spend time in any of the chakras, and multiple chakras may be active at the same time even when our awareness is only in a specific one. Most people spend a bit of time in the "root," which is the 1st chakra. We're there when doing generic human activities such as sleeping or eating, and when doing activities for which we are so conditioned that we do not think about them. Beyond that, each of us varies. The highest chakras are likely the least active except for a person with special training. Overall, our upbringing, personality, culture, and spiritual life will greatly influence where our consciousness lies.

We can show how we are spending our time over a 24-hour day using a pie chart. The two pie charts below compare two random people, Joan and Thomas, who are pretty different.

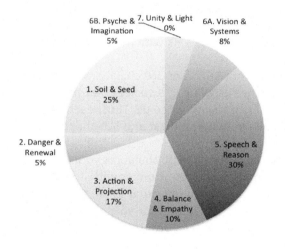

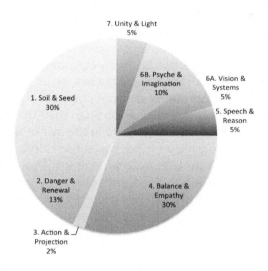

Joan is a reasonable, sophisticated, and empowered scientist with a focus on life's practicalities. She avoids anything too disorienting, suppresses past traumas, and lacks experience with body-mind or spiritual practices. She spends a lot of time being a rational problemsolver, and she suffers occasional explosive fits and strong bias on certain topics. She is a paragon of society's progress, but some chakras are underused.

Thomas is a quiet, loving, and simple-living monk, committed to daily spiritual practices including meditation and body work to locate and shed false attachments. He takes a loose approach to self-improvement, rejects scientism, and avoids occasions of bias. He also spends a lot of time using "active imagination" to explore new ideas. Though his body-mind practices touch all the chakras, he still has issues and feet in the world.

Your Lesson Zone

As a species, as a culture, and as individuals, we are in multiple chakras at once. As we will explore in the next section, Jung observed that humanity as a whole is in the lowest chakra, while our modern societies promote the 5th chakra, and individuals can be anywhere.

Humanity: As a species, we persist in a material world. If we lose our physical bodies, our food, or air, death results and only dust and echoes remain. Thus, all of us are anchored in the 1st chakra, our shared soil—and like an uprooted tree, we cannot survive otherwise.

Society: Society is our shared norms, practices, institutions, and expectations. Some say society is a kind of mass hypnosis. Much of the civilized world today promotes the 5th chakra, which Jung links to air, speech, reason, and the throat. Society upholds dialogue, education, knowledge, and a broad, objective distance. Even this book is words. This 5th chakra is society's *ideal*. Of course, individuals often use this chakra poorly, and then society falters. Diplomacy is a favored route to conflict resolution, but violence persists. Objectivity is a favored route to wisdom, but addictive worship of "idols" and ideologies easily pull us down. At best, history is a long walk with many detours and failures while also vigilantly cultivating a higher standard.

You: Individuals are in various places, though usually in the 2nd or 3rd chakras. We are all born like sprouting seeds of potential in the 1st chakra, and we grow up in a society that may, or may not, successfully propel us up to the 5th chakra. Many local factors influence us. Thus, each of us, individually, is somewhere in the awakening process, usually between the 1st and 5th chakras and very rarely higher, since societies seldom provide tools to go further.

Your Lesson Zone: Presently, you are likely focusing on one specific chakra as your *lesson zone*. You are exploring this chakra in order to learn something. If you are younger with less life experience, this is likely a lower chakra. If you are older with significant life experience, this is likely a middle chakra. Rarely are persons focusing on a higher chakra. The details for your personal lesson are mostly unconscious because your ego blocks out the pain of encountering and dealing with it, but as you read, you will likely resonate with one chakra as your current lesson zone. From that chakra, you can reach out to adjacent chakras—the next-down lower chakra as a familiar and trusted resource, and the next-up higher chakra as an aspiration for your future.

Kundalini Yoga: We are usually taught that consciousness is in the head. However, as we'll soon see through Jung's eyes, many people are cut off from the lower chakras, unable to feel thoroughly, and thus unable to honestly evaluate themselves, much less realize their potential. We suffer emotional blockages. We hold to false attachments, unconscious addictions, and manufactured identifications. We shut out these things, ironically thinking we are above them in the 5th or 6th chakras. Happily, kundalini yoga helps us become aware of and release these challenges, to open, clear, and align the chakras. This is why chakra work starts in the lowest, most physical practices, using breath and movement to reconnect the head to the body. Then we work upward from the root chakra to the crown chakra, helping us locate the healthiest expression of all the chakras.

Part 2

Explore the Chakras

For each chakra, you will find a snapshot, a detailed explanation with quotes from Jung, suggested exercises, and more. **Bolded text** highlights key points. Most people find the exercises clarify how the chakras play out in a practical way in everyday life. You will be able to rate each chakra. At the end of this section, you can view all the chakras at once. They appear as snapshots and as symbolic tableaus. You may collect your ratings into one chart for broader reflection and to identify where you might focus going forward.

1st Chakra*
Soil & Seed

*you exist
you have potential*

> This is your *root* chakra. Like the earth, it lends support. You use it to stay grounded in your body and to meet your basic material needs. When used in a balanced way, you stay in synch with your physical environment, find comfort in the familiar, and enjoy a secure place you can call home. This chakra also links to cultural norms, attention to factual practicalities, and the blueprint of your potential. Overuse of this chakra invites materialism, lack of self-awareness, and disinterest in change beyond day-to-day activities.

Called *mūlādhāra* in Sanskrit, this first chakra represents our basic bodily existence on the planet. It means "root support" and usually links to the element of earth, evoking images of mountains, fields, deserts, caves, and such. Earth has qualities like strength, endurance, and stability, and it begs questions like whether a soil is more fertile or barren. Jung explains how this chakra anchors us in the mundane, and the quality of "soil" we find ourselves in impacts all facets of our lives.

This chakra is like a seed in soil. We each begin life literally as a mere embryo; from there we "sprout" and grow, and we are necessarily fused with the world at first. That is, we start living within a physical environment, society, and culture. We originate there and differentiate from it later. It is child-like, even innocent, and includes all the assumptions and physical needs we are born into, before something challenges us to grow. Think of how many popular stories often start with a youth's naïve life of simple labors before a harsh danger stirs things up and awakens him or her to action and growth to become a hero. As Jung pointed out, in classic Hindu symbology a huge gray elephant represents this chakra. This great beast is social with incredible carrying power, a profound memory, and a gentle demeanor until provoked. This is the elephantine power of the physical world and our origins, for good and ill. It is our home-base, whether or not it is warm and reassuring.

When we are rooted in this chakra, our viewpoint is focused outward and limited to our current superficial reality. We are unaware of our psychological potential, defense mechanisms, and other hidden dramas—and when such phenomena are pointed out, we easily dismiss them out of hand. Jung says of this chakra, "the gods are asleep," meaning our psyche is hidden and our

* Jung's discussion of this first chakra is notably more abstract than the others.

1st Chakra: Soil & Seed
We are born and grow from the Earth and its bounty, learning cultural
and family traditions, and to earth we must return.

unique potential is "but a germ." We are "not yet born" and we sleep "in the roots of the world." The word *kundal* in kundalini means "coiled up," referring to energy potential that sleeps within us, both psychologically and physically at the base of the spine. The purpose of yoga is to awaken this energy source, to move us up out of this chakra and make "the gods" (the actors on our psyche's stage) active in our lives to challenge us. In yoga, the word *buddhi* refers to one's personal consciousness, while kundalini refers to everything else (that's impersonal); and Jung states, "Kundalini represents the development of that impersonal life." So there's a paradox. Un-fusing a person from his or her root existence involves a universal journey, and the person's end point (in the highest chakra) is a return to the universal pool of the Divine from which he or she was born.

We can visualize this 1st chakra as a great bowl or shell that contains all the other chakras. Wherever we go, we are in it, because it contains everything else we do. Adults often see themselves well beyond this chakra, and modern societies certainly seek to stand tall and see widely with reason, science, and technology. But Jung counsels that this rosy view of adulthood is an illusion. He says, "You can imagine the cosmic chakra system as an immense skyscraper whose foundations go deep down in the earth and contain six cellars, one above the other. One could then go from the first up to the sixth cellar, but one would still find oneself in the depths of the earth. This whole cellar system is the cosmic *mūlādhāra*." Thus, even after we have reached the highest chakra, we still find ourselves here. And there is both a personal version of this chakra, which is the soil we sprout and grow from, and also a universal version of this chakra, which is the soil for all human beings. To think we can escape this chakra, Jung says, is to "confuse the personal with the cosmic."

What does this mean in practice? **Whatever the norms of a society, that is the base level of consciousness**. In the words of British philosopher Alan W. Watts, "We are living in a culture entirely hypnotized by the illusion of time, in which the so-called present moment is felt as nothing but an infinitesimal hairline between an all-powerfully causative past and an absorbingly important future. We have no present. Our consciousness is almost completely preoccupied with memory and expectation. We do not realize that there never was, is, nor will be any other experience than present experience. We are therefore out of touch with reality. We confuse the world as talked about, described, and measured with the world which actually is." Thus, if an activity is routine or habitual, you're feeding this chakra. If you're borrowing or transmitting a label, idea, or factoid given to you by someone else without investigating it or trying it out for yourself in some way, you're likely in this chakra. Even when we are speaking about religion, science, or philosophy and we feel informed but are merely following what others have given to us, then we are still in this chakra.

Perhaps surprisingly, **Jung encourages us to embrace this chakra and take it seriously**. He says, "You must believe in this world, make roots, do the best you can, even if you have to believe in the most absurd things—to believe, for instance, that this world is very definite, that it matters absolutely whether such-and-such a treaty is made or not," whatever degree you earn, job you take, house you buy, person you marry, and kids you have (or not). Even when a particular task feels absurd or spiritually pointless, he encourages us to try. "It may be completely futile, but you have to believe in it, have to make it almost a religious conviction, merely for the purpose of putting your signature under the treaty, so that trace is left of you." For emphasis, he adds, "For you should leave some trace in this world which notifies that you have been here, that something has happened."

But why? Jung's answer is not about being worldly, significant, or even heeding a calling to a cause greater than ourselves, which are parts of later chakras. Instead, **we need this chakra to grow psychologically.** He explains, "It is utterly important that one should be in this world," to fulfill "the germ of life which one is." So we need a nourishing soil to grow. "You see," he says, "the shoot must come out of the ground, and if the personal spark has never gotten into the ground, nothing will come out of it." The soil is where we actualize our potential. He adds, let's say you experience a peak moment or a realization, but you do not actualize it in your everyday life, then you "simply are thrown back, and nothing has happened; it is an absolutely valueless experience." Worse, when we do not have our feet on the ground, we can easily fool ourselves. We may try to divert our instinctual impulses and practical needs into something higher, maybe more socially acceptable or productive toward some goal—even a spiritual goal. But Jung says, "That idea, that we can sublimate ourselves and become entirely spiritual and no air is left"—to float off into outer space—that "is an inflation." By inflation he means an exaggerated self-importance or a delusion of success.

While we need soil to grow, we cannot remain in the soil or it will smother us. The yoga framework says we experience the world in a distorted away through blinders and lenses, and we stare helplessly at things projected our way that capture our attention and drive us in whatever directions the world is going. Consider a baby: from birth he or she only experiences what family and the local environment present. Those inputs shape the baby's mind and views, which might not fit the wider reality or his or her personal potential. In Hinduism, this situation is called *māyā*, where the norms and concerns of the world are like a magic show where things are not what they seem. Or, more subtly, something exists, but it is constantly changing and hides the doorways to a spiritual life. In Jung's terms, *māyā* is like a magic trick being played on us by "the gods"—the hidden actors in our psyche. The growth process, which we can call "awakening," involves perceiving and confronting these little gods and transmuting them. Without starting the growth process, Jung says we remain just a seed, unborn.

Alas, Jung says, "**There are plenty of people who are not yet born.**" He explains, "They seem to be all here, they walk about—but as a matter of fact, they are not yet born." Actually, "They are in the world only on parole and are soon to be returned to … where they started originally"; "they have not formed a connection with this world"; they "are just identical," and are "living the provisional life, a conditioned life, the life of somebody who is still connected by an umbilical cord as thick as a ship's rope." And we are not mere accidental victims of this. Rather, Jung says, "we are entangled in the roots, and we ourselves are the roots." We *are* a part of the world. "We make roots, we cause roots to be, we are rooted in the soil, and there is no getting away for us, because we must be there as long as we live."

How do we safely move out of the confines of this chakra? It is like quicksand. Jung suggests, "we must invent a new scheme." He says that if you succeed in actualizing your potential, your "shoot will come up from the ground; namely, that possibility of a detachment from this world—from the world of *māyā*." In mythology, opening Pandora's box or eating forbidden fruit takes us out of the 1st chakra and into the next one. Moreover, as organisms, given minimal nourishment we naturally start to grow, to accumulate problems, and we tend to search for answers. In kundalini, breathing and other practices are meant to pull us out of our heads, away from *māyā*, and into the tangible present moment. Energy moving up from this lowest chakra is a tangible sign of success. Whatever the means, Jung believes there is an innate push, and he says, after "you touch the reality in which you live, and stay for several decades if you leave your trace, then the impersonal process can begin."

Get Grounded

Here are some mindful activities for this chakra to cultivate a supportive material environment.

1. **Check with reality.** Take stock of your material needs and the facts of your current situation. What's in your bank account? How's your health? Who are you spending time with? When looking for solutions, focus on facts "on the ground" and tangible, material resources you can tap.
2. **Question assumptions.** Just because you grew up a certain way or most people follow a norm doesn't mean it works for you. If you engage in a daily habit or follow a belief that you haven't examined yet, consider researching it, briefly setting it aside as a test, and/or reflecting on its tangible impact.
3. **Shed excess possessions.** Sort through what you have accumulated and donate or sell excess material goods. Similarly, whenever you shop, consider if you truly need something that attracts your attention. Focus more on what creates growth experiences rather than mere display.
4. **Live in healthy spaces.** Stake out a healthy physical environment for the purpose of work, learning, and as a home. No matter how small or large, find a personal space for yourself that's free of stressors. Whenever you can, schedule regular retreats into nature or beautiful spaces, such as going to the beach or hiking.
5. **Put down roots.** Make a place you can call home, a familiar nest, where you have roots and feel safe and comfortable. Fill it with rich memories and signs of your successes. This space nourishes you and links to the earth and to those who have come before you (your family and ancestors).
6. **During meditation or yoga**, connect to the earth. Breathe in deeply down to your belly and focus on the earth as your support. Draw on images and feelings of the natural world—all that is timeless and strong. When standing, root your feet into the ground. When moving, let your legs and pelvis lead you (rather than your belly, chest, or head). Practice staying silent.
7. **Give thanks each day** for your meals and other material benefits in your life. Focus on what you have rather than what you lack. Desire is a cause of suffering, and a great way to show thanks for material comfort and success is to personally share some of that with others in need.

How grounded are you currently? Count how much you identified above: 1   2   3   4   5   6   7

1ST CHAKRA: SOIL & SEED

Jung drew on symbols to help people get in touch with themselves and resolve their issues. You can do that too. Refer to the tableau and exercises below to explore how you use this chakra.

— Walk solid with feet on the ground
— Healthy pride of heritage
— Harmony with parents
— Comfortable place to call home
— Enjoy being in nature (with plants, animals, etc)
— Attend to factual practicalities
— Content with life's daily essentials
— Access to resources
— Align with life's cycles and seasons

The outer frame is the whole material world and one's culture. Within, the circle stands for female wholeness while the tiered pyramid stands for male hierarchy. The main cavity is a cave, ovum, or womb with cords or roots. Within it lies a seed, embryo, or the unrealized individual. Below, a spring with three-and-one-half spirals symbolizes latent kundalini energy. The doors are a birth canal or exit to the surface, where one can slowly advance. The eye is one's badge of cultural affiliation. The mother gives birth to us, while the elephant carries tradition. The *ankh* means we return to the soil at death.

Looking at the tableau, what comes to mind? What memories does it evoke? Or consider, what meanings or stories does it inspire? You might meditate quietly on the image, perhaps with a question also in mind. Or feel free to draw your own symbolic version of this chakra.

At times, the modern world can feel as if it has no past and its foundations keep shifting like quicksand. To find stability, dig into your family line and your society's history and culture—ideally, centuries back—and locate the places, practices, and principles that have benefitted your life now.

2nd Chakra
Danger & Renewal

you feel
you adjust and explore

This is your *sacral* chakra. Like water, it is essential for growth. You use it to stay connected to yourself and to others through shared experiences. When used in a balanced way, you keep up good health habits, stay in touch with your body cycles and emotional responses, and easily enjoy others' company, including close contact. Water also prompts adventures, spurs your potential through reflection, and is a place of renewal. Imbalance invites disconnection, low self-esteem, and ill health from pent-up stress, hurt, and anger.

Jung links this center to the *svādhishthāna* chakra and the element of water. It sits below the naval and near the kidneys, intestines, and womb. In mythology and in many religions, water has multiple meanings—from the amniotic sack and baptism to drowning and sea monsters. However it appears, Jung linked this chakra to the first budding of consciousness and a fear of ego loss. We face death, real or symbolic, and in doing so, realize our own life, emerging with a renewed sense of value and a clearer purpose as we start our journey into consciousness.

Water is essential for life. Think of all the ways we encounter it. First there is the womb. Similarly, a seed in the earth needs water to sprout and grow. Sometimes we must apply extra water, as in arid conditions, while at other times the climate is just right, or even excessively wet. In the same way, what "waters" you? What sustains your core psychological needs? This chakra space offers us refreshment, nurturing, and cleansing. Without it, we tend to shrivel up. This is particularly true when a chakra is "blocked" or "contaminated"—when it is a well that does not produce the waters we need.

Jung's approach to this chakra is mythical. He proposes there is a push by the unconscious to cleanse. As if called by a siren's song or by happy memories of our mother's womb, we go into the water. Jung suggests we might enter for a ritual baptism, as Jesus did with John the Baptist. Or we might simply seek calm in a relaxing space. Jung recalls the legendary Gilgamesh, who dives into the sea in search of a plant that grants immortality. It is a place of adventure. Or, like the Bible's Jonah, we might be caught by a storm and flung into the sea as a divine test. We might even be like the Egyptians

2nd Chakra: Danger & Renewal
We can dive deep to face dangers, mysteries, and fears as we use our
talents, search for treasure, and gain renewal.

chasing after the Hebrews into the Red Sea, seeing victory but finding calamity. In modern films, characters may transgress societal limits, such as taking a late-night swim in a lake labeled "No Trespassing." Whatever the action, we are out of our element—we are not sea born—and there is danger. In kundalini symbology, that danger is symbolized by a *makara*, a leviathan that may drown and devour us.

In modern life **we often find ourselves inundated by this center—caught in its whirlpool—whenever solid earth gives way or we go thirsty far too long, or we tire of the fires of the next chakra center**. The break might be sudden, like a car accident, death of a loved one, or a cancer diagnosis. Or we might suffer a suffocating weight that subtly builds every day, such as from discrimination, poverty, or echoes of childhood abuse; we shoulder it, take it into our gut, and seal it off, locking it into our body, and slowly it ravages us with anxiety, depression, guilt, and shame. Inevitably, when we become aware that something is wrong, we feel a growing urge to break free, to vomit up the toxins, to swim up to the surface to freedom, to live on our own terms.

Modern life stresses us. It keeps us in high gear. The baseline of urban life in particular tends to be fast, loud, ugly, miasmic, and distracting. Retreat to a quiet mountain cabin and whole foods for six months and see your baseline down-shift to a new normal. Stress puts us in a fight-or-flight mode, and chronic stress leads to disease—physical, emotional, mental, or spiritual. To deal with dis-ease, we can turn to hiking, massage, swimming or such—all good stuff. Or we might use alcohol, cannabis, caffeine, ecstasy, nicotine, painkillers or sleeping pills to loosen up or get numb. We might get violent, self-harm, or do extreme sports to feel alive. These all have genuine uses, and compared to the 1st chakra, these raise consciousness, but over time we may become addicted, stuck in this chakra's vortex, and yearn to "get clean."

A practical aspect of this chakra is that **it grants awareness of psyche as expressed via the body**. We notice the knot in our stomach, stirrings of the sex urge, a spring in our step, and so forth. This center doesn't analyze these sensations. Rather, it alerts us to important situations. The stomach knot tells us something is wrong, regardless of words and appearances. Unless the loins stir, there is no actual sexual chemistry. In order to practice kundalini yoga effectively—recognizing the chakras as more than an idea, to move energy for our growth—we must awaken this center. More broadly, to truly learn anything, to know it in our gut and in our bones, we must feel it in the lower body and lock it in.

If we want to learn anything deeply, we learn it here. Jung recalls the "primitive method of the schoolmasters fifty years ago," which he experienced. He says, "We were taught the ABCs with a whip. We were eight boys sitting on one bench, and the schoolmaster had a whip of willow wands, just long enough to touch all the backs at once. He said, 'This is A' (bang), 'This is B' (bang). You see, causing a physical sensation was the old method of teaching. It was not very painful because when he beat on the eight backs at the same time you just cringed and didn't feel it very much. But it makes an impression; the boys were actually sitting up and listening." Jung contrasts his experience with the modern method typical of the higher chakras, where the teacher says, "Will you be kind enough to pay attention, please?" Jung connects the lash to societies that inflict wounds in initiations. When the elders hand over mystical tribal secrets, they also "make cuts and rub ashes into [the youth], or they starve the initiates, they do not let them sleep, or frighten them out of their wits. Then they give the teaching, and it catches hold of them because it has gone in with physical discomfort or pain." Today, the military still uses these techniques to help ingrain knowledge as automatic and instinctual.

In terms of development, our dominant psychological "function" shines in this center as a means to prosper. We differentiate ourselves from the world, which we got to know well in the 1st chakra. We use our dominant function, our favorite way of being, to deal with unpleasant circumstances, strive for better, and generally manage our lives beyond basic human functions. When we leave home and go to school, we find ways to learn and get along with others beyond our genetic programming. Research with identical twins raised apart suggests that our psychological preferences are half nature and half nurture. Jung himself said that we develop a dominant function as a way of managing at least three different demands: Our basic human nature, our particular genetic endowments including talents; and our culture's task areas such as schooling, military service, marriage, and job expectations*.

This chakra is home to self-consciousness, an early facet of consciousness. In addition to sexual development, young adults in their early teens go through an awkward phase. They are acutely self-aware of how they appear to the larger world. This includes anything related to them such as parents, home, hobbies, and friends. They feel acutely too. A social *faux pas* or athletic failure might become a mountain of embarrassment. These years tax us physically, socially, and cognitively. The person's dominant function must shine and act as a steady anchor as other functions start to slowly develop. And all along, the young man or woman is half-aware of this process. **Choices made as an adolescent tend to seal themselves into the body**. Imagine a pal in middle school drawing you close in friendship and then whispering a nasty put-down that stays with you, impacting self-esteem. Compensating for these half-aware choices and impacts in later life can be challenging, even from the highest chakras.

Though Jung didn't mention it, ***kundalini* yoga links this chakra with sexuality**. Sex is more than an urge or immediate survival issue. It requires union with someone else to generate new life, a new person who starts a new spiritual journey in the 1st chakra. More broadly, **sex exposes us psychologically in a very intimate way**. We may experience the joy of renewal, the danger of violence and abuse, or anything in between. As with other aspects of this chakra, sexual experiences are deeply imprinted into the body, such that gender roles, family life, and relationships later in life are deeply impacted. Thus, throughout our lives, this center strongly influences how we connect with others, how we choose relationships, and how we perceive and define our social and sexual experiences.

Jung explores this chakra's spiritual dimension. In Christianity, he says, **"the world is only a preparation for a higher condition**, and the here and now, the state of being involved in this world, is error and sin. The sacraments and rites of the early church all meant freeing man from the merely personal state of mind and allowing him to participate symbolically in a higher condition. In the mystery of baptism—the plunge into *svādhishthāna*—the 'old Adam' dies and the 'spiritual man' is born. The transfiguration and ascension of Christ is the symbolical representation and anticipation of the desired end, that is, being lifted above the personal and into the supra-personal. In the old church Christ represents the leader, and hence the promise of what the mystic or initiate could also

* *Psychological Types* by C. G. Jung. Princeton University Press, 1976.

contain." Thus, the early church's rites and mystical elements were aids to pushing out of mundane life to live a more Christ-like life, and in the process, become more awake, more conscious.

In today's busy mental lives, we may forget this chakra. Therapeutic practices like yoga aim to expose and release our addictions and baggage—to help us purge pains and make room for pure sweat water. Sometimes we need to thoroughly empty ourselves, to hit rock bottom, before we can take on something new. The baggage we carry may not even be ours, and without cleansing, we may move in and out of this chakra throughout our days without appreciating its influence, forever held back by issues that talk and drugs cannot reach, as we keep yearning for renewal and hope.

Get Vibrant
Here are some mindful activities with this chakra to cultivate vibrant health and happiness.

1. **Nurture your body**. Shift away from addictive behaviors, away from stimulants and depressants such as sugar, alcohol, and party drugs. At the same time, move toward healthy alternatives such as exercise, gardening, massage, meditation, organic food, moving music, and yoga.

2. **Listen to your gut**. Heed your gut response to people and situations. What "triggers" you? Take time to locate and release physical-emotional blockages in your body, such as situations that stress your stomach or past traumatic events stored in the abdomen. Holding in or ignoring "baggage" is more taxing than releasing it. Physical therapy can help you here.

3. **Be with safe people**. Surround yourself with others of mutual trust and respect. When unsure, look at people's actions and how you feel around them more than their words. Gently exit toxic relationships. As part of this, engage in healthy sexual interactions that satisfy both partners.

4. **Cultivate the arts and adventure**. Look for ways to challenge your body and mind in order to stay fresh and youthful. A stimulated mind and active body keeps us young. Try the performing arts, such as dance. Or just play outside. Consider travel, workshops, and new hobbies. You do not need to commit—just explore. Sometimes, adventure means going outside your comfort zone.

5. **Renew your environment**. Run an air purifier. Replace plastics and toxic materials with natural ones. Shut out mechanical urban noises and add nature sounds. You might set up a little waterfall. Favor natural beauty and elegant design over ugly distractions.

6. **During meditation or yoga**, connect to your gut. Feel out areas of tightness, restricted breathing, or waves of herky-jerky motion that come after intense focus. With care for yourself, gently bring up triggers and negative memories, and use breath and motion to help release them. When standing or moving, practice slow graceful movements. Practice a gentle but deep voice.

7. **Give thanks each day** to the supportive people in your life. Recall what they've said or done that you are grateful for. Remember, it takes 5 positives to counter 1 negative! Include anyone who helps in your daily routine such as grocers even if they aren't acquaintances.

How vibrant are you currently? Count how much you identified above: 1   2   3   4   5   6   7

2ND CHAKRA: DANGER & RENEWAL

Jung drew on symbols to help people get in touch with themselves and resolve their issues. You can do that too. Refer to the tableau and exercises below to explore how you use this chakra.

— Curious with a drive to explore
— Solve puzzles and assess dangers well
— Harmony with friends
— Aware of and adjust to how others' perceive and react to you
— Physically fit with healthy lifestyle
— Tap your talents
— Participate in male/female sex roles
— Emotional maturity, few hang-ups, deal with baggage

At center, the young ego sails a boat. The *makara* (monster) prowls below. Chests on the sea floor are a trap, a treasure, and trash (hidden baggage). The ego has a spear (its talent), and it must dive with it and explore to get the treasure. Islands on the side, like faces, suggest self-conscious awareness of others' stares and also sex roles and relations. Both, half-submerged, hold sexual allure. The world is full of life: We can plant, catch, grow, and/or create. In the sky, the sun, moon, star, and cloud are nature's touchstones. The big frame is the world, one's body, and also one's psyche.

Looking at the tableau, what comes to mind? What memories does it evoke? Or consider, what meanings or stories does it inspire? You might meditate quietly on the image, perhaps with a question in mind. Or feel free to draw your own version of this chakra.

How do you manage your "baggage?" You can bury it, though it will likely eat at you. You can channel it into creative projects. You can mask or relieve it with drugs, exercise, or massage. You can analyze it to find lessons. Or you can weaponize it to rage at others. Now, how can you get healthier?

3rd Chakra
Action & Projection

you struggle
you act with confidence

This is your *solar plexus* chakra. Like a fire, it sets you alight with idealism. You use it to energetically advance an empowering truth, mission, or cause. When used in a balanced way, you stand tall with confidence, know your values and beliefs, and easily stay brave and strong to advance your calling or goals. Fire also warms and illuminates, burns away all that's rubbish, and is a sign of civilization. Overuse of this chakra invites fanaticism, mythologizing of people and objects into angels and demons, and blindness to one's own faults.

This chakra center, called *manipūra*, links to the element of fire. *Manipūra* means "jeweled fortress" or "the fullness of jewels." It sits at our solar plexus and near the stomach, which breaks down food, and near the adrenal glands, which build our muscles and power our fight response. Here, we are energized toward goals but also prone to conflict. We are alight with "The Truth" and revere holiness but are terrified of demons and heretics. We easily singe ourselves and others. Jung expounded on this center. It is a powerful and dangerous space that dominates much of human activity.

When we are born, we emerge from a watery womb into the light of a harsh world. In this new world we are easily disturbed and we lash out, like fire, to destroy any irritants and to satiate our desires. As Jung points out, this chakra also links to the sun and re-birth in myth and religion. **When reborn, we start a new kind of existence** with an eternal soul ("eternal flame") and may start with a different name and even a new family. We join something larger than ourselves, with a purpose and mission. We reorient to an "energizing abstraction" that we worship or deify that allows us to escape the futility of personal existence into the promise of an eternal existence. Often there are clear changes in our goals, philosophy, and behavior when this happens. This rebirth may be religious or secular. Either way, it is extreme. As a modern example, *Star Wars* represented this idea in the "Light Side of the Force" versus the "Dark Side of the Force". We are called to pick sides and fight.

Several clues signal when this chakra is active. First and foremost, **we are highly energized, but we also aggressively push down some parts of ourselves while projecting our unconscious parts onto the world**. As a result, we can be rigid, vigilant, and judgmental. We pick fights as we engage

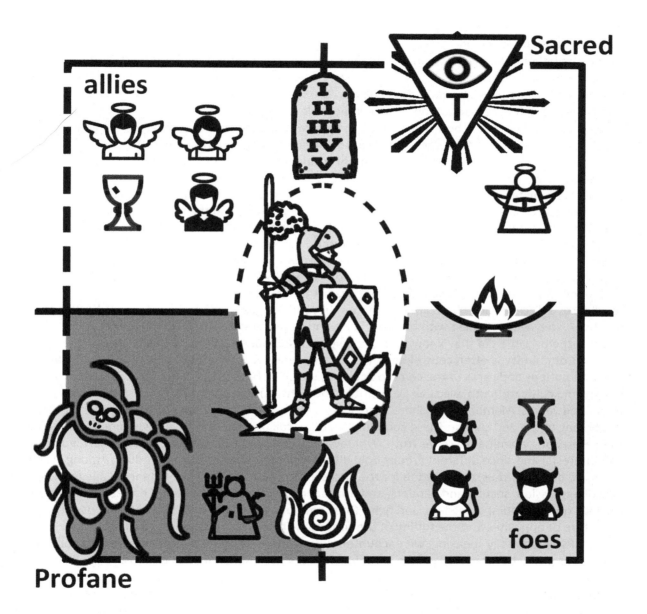

3rd Chakra: Action & Projection
With Truth as a guide star, we are energized to take action toward
goals, though we can get extreme, demonizing and idolizing.

our opposite, seeking to slay anything that represents the Other, our old life or "demons"—people or desires that hinder salvation. We view all this conflict as making way for progress, for as Jung repeats, "war is the father of all things." In this center, we are also prone to think with our solar plexus, to shout and grab, and suffer explosions—"sex, power, every devil in our nature gets loose." We are filled with shoulds, wants, and needs because this chakra is "the source of desire, the whole emotional world." Ultimately, our lofty goals and standards are impossible to sustain. For somebody caught in this center, Jung quotes the Buddha: "The whole world is in flames, your ears, your eyes, everywhere you pour out the fire of desire, and that is the fire of illusion because you desire things which are futile."

On the plus side, like the radiant sun, **this chakra is a source of illumination, empowerment, and passion**. We strive to make ourselves and the world better, even if we are misguided. Jung doesn't mention falling in love, but consider all the ways we place upon a pedestal those we admire, projecting our desires for an idealized union. The resulting vision, and the conflict it creates, makes us feel alive even though the person we "love" cannot live up to the mythic role we give them. The Bible offers many examples of this chakra's intense dramas. For example, the otherwise pious King David seduced the beautiful Bathsheba and then saved her from punishment for adultery by sending her husband Uriah to certain death in battle. He is torn between his own selfish desires and his genuine zeal to follow divine edicts that act as a ward against the consequences of unchecked desires. Or recall Jesus's disciples after he visited them from beyond the grave. "They saw tongues like flames of a fire ... they were all filled with the Holy Spirit and began to speak in other tongues as the Spirit enabled them." Little did they know then the unique tribulations awaiting each of them.

Community is often central here. Necessarily, when we are reborn, we are set apart from the assumptions and cares of the common culture, which lie back in the 1st chakra. To sustain our energy and cultivate Truth, we seek like-spirited and right-minded persons. The community is a castle for shared values. Members may share a language, race, sex or such, though mere physical similarities belong to the 2nd chakra. These communities often call on members to leave behind family—possibly even betray family—to serve Truth. Whatever the community, it fosters shared beliefs, goals, and interests; and since different groups hold different values, conflict is a by-product. Among groups there are different idols, competition for resources, perceptions of aggression, tangled allegiances, acts of aggression, secrets and blinders, and drives for power and domination. Communities demonize each other, appoint crusaders, and fight. One community may win for a time, but the psychological nature of opposites and the futility of the supposed Truth ensures conflicts continue.

Psychologically speaking, **we encounter our unconscious in this center, but we also polarize its parts as perfect or terrible, and we erect barriers against it** so it does not burn us. Jung observed how these barriers take many forms. We invent rites, rituals, rules, protocols, customs, mantras, old sayings, slogans, and similar defenses. This chakra's symbolic animal is the ram: an object of sacrifice to appease the Divine. If the sacrifice is done by the rules, then success; otherwise, disaster may occur. Indeed, we are always taking care. We whisper about Truths—a holy flame, G-d's name, or the Biblical Ark of the Covenant—because they are too "hot" to touch directly and rules will keep us safe. Similarly, we "speak obliquely about sin and failure" and hypocrisy, so that we do not invite in evil. While these examples are religious, secular ideologies have their own "holy" mantras, relics, and rituals. Whatever the protocols to manage our unconscious desires and fears, such barriers guide and support willpower, and they hold back anger and "a thousand other emotions" like a pressure cooker. A society might allow ritual combat, self-flagellation, exhausting coming-of-age trials, and so forth as ways to release steam and prevent explosions of fighting, destruction, and killing.

Today's world is ripe with action and projection, where the ends justify the means in the name of power or progress. Some may survive cut-off from power, sacrificing faith in order to avoid error. A few others utterly embrace war or a violent, radicalized ideology based in the solar plexus—with shouting, rioting, and destruction. But **for most of us**, **the purveyors of television, politics, and the infotainment industry stoke this chakra** day and night. They aim to excite our senses and desires in order to profit themselves. They rile us up, divide us against each other, and present images of jewels that titillate our passions. All of it is manufactured, where celebrities take on the roles that temple idols played in prior eras. They are presented in a way that mesmerizes and is glamorous. The original meaning of the word *glamor* is an illusion, deceit or distraction. We speak of "fans" today, forgetting the word means "fanatical." Jung lived before our media age bloomed fully, and he did not comment on it in these lectures. This is just my own observation, but it seems to fit.

We tend to blindly err in perception and judgment when caught in this chakra. For example, we overlook the faults of whatever we idealize or make holy, or we chalk up faults to unusual circumstances or a rare and trivial event. In contrast, the faults of those we vilify are exploded from molehills into mountains. Our foe suffers from vile character, hopeless stupidity, hatred, or a lethal weaknesses that is a threat to everyone. This is called the Fundamental Attribution Error, and this chakra is prone to an unending litany of such errors. The great error is that the Truth is obvious and we are perfectly rational and wise while the Other is irrational, stupid, and perhaps evil.

This center is where **we consciously experience and embrace our strengths and the power of ego.** We get to know our core needs and values and we strive to express our preferred way of perceiving and deciding things. For many people, when they discover their "true calling" or "true self," they experience a profound rush of energy. They no longer feel lost, odd or "just a chip off the old block." They find validation and receive a title or label. They celebrate their nature. In contrast, that person's non-preferences remain mysterious. The person might say, "I'm very open! No wonder I don't like my boss; she's very closed." The differences can leave us anxious even if we wish to be tolerant. Or we idealize the person, perhaps irrationally. Someone might say, "I'm very emotional. But my partner is a genius with math and science unlike me, so very rational." This is stereotyping and over-simplifying with boxes, even when we mean well. More plainly, we know we're here when we over-play our preferences, hate on others who aren't like us, or use dehumanizing terms like "them."

Our **behavior here often comes from a well-meaning place.** After all, we're sharing the fruit of a great insight! But imagine a person has a major life-changing experience—say, the divine unity of the crown chakra—and then returns to the grind of daily life. He or she might have to survive for years off the fumes of that wonderful hour. This is particularly true when the experience was random, without means to revisit that higher chakra. Instead, the 2nd chakra is tasked with locking rebirth into the body while this chakra is tasked with providing ongoing energy and direction, perhaps through rituals, rules, and campaigns against the opposition.

In day-to-day life, we are here whenever we get caught in a fiery tornado of psychological projection. To quote a Japanese phrase, we're here when "our stomach stands up" as we face down demons that are exaggerated reflections of our own adolescent impulses, dark urges, and ugly failings. Jung states that **even when we do not spend a lot of time in this chakra, we may experience eruptions** of emotion and opinion that smolder like old fires from the past.

Get Empowered

Here are some mindful activities with this chakra to cultivate an empowered life based in values.

1. **Focus on strengths**. Identify and develop your talents. Your talents are where you shine and gain rewards just by doing them. These are your birthright, and when you build on them, you really shine as exceptional. If you are currently using your talents, great. If not, or if you notice a talent that's going untapped, find a way to bring it into your life.
2. **Identify ideals and goals**. What does your ideal world look like? Consider what you are passionate about and how to manifest that. What steps will it take to get to that world? You might start with the finished picture and work backward. There are your goals and sign-posts to success.
3. **Be resourceful**. Pay attention to your gut, what excites and motives you, and what helps you "walk tall" so that you speak and act with confidence, energy, resonance, and resilience. Also, keep looking around for resources: people, ideas, practices, and tools that help you progress and stay strong. To get these, you might need to go on a pilgrimage of sorts.
4. **Join a community**. Locate a group of like hearts and minds. This might be a circle of friends, colleagues, or fellow faithful. Work with others to promote your shared values and build toward shared goals. Avoid getting mired in pettiness and gossip and stay focused on commonalities.
5. **Tame the myth-making**. Name the mythic roles that you project onto others, including people and groups you do not know such as celebrities and politicians. Trust that they are human like you, not monsters or saviors. Take off the "myth lens" by listing your commonalities as well as differences.
6. **During meditation or yoga**, bring your hands to your solar plexus. You can rub your palms to warm them, or make a fist of your right hand and cup it in your left, drawing them to you. Visualize fingers as flames. When standing and moving, stay erect and confidently focus on ways to build, heal, and help using your unique gifts, to constructively improve yourself or a situation.
7. **Give thanks each day** to something larger than yourself. Be thankful for your talents, successes, and lessons gained from set-backs. Find ways to regularly reconnect with your values, re-energize yourself, and stay true to your goals through mutual aid, prayer, and other practices.

How empowered are you currently? Count how much you identified above: 1 2 3 4 5 6 7

3RD CHAKRA: ACTION & PROJECTION

Jung drew on symbols to help people get in touch with themselves and resolve their issues. You can do that too. Refer to the tableau and exercises below to explore how you use this chakra.

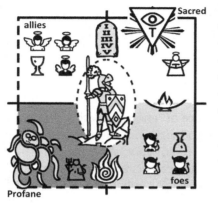

— Know your identity and values
— Energized to take action
— Life holds meaning and purpose
— Confidently move toward goals/ideals
— Stand firm for what matters to you
— Identify foes/allies without making them into idols, angels, or demons
— Part of an intentional community
— Stay informed without falling prey to slogans and wishful thinking

"Truth" breaks the outer frame in the upper right corner. Truth is an all-seeing eye that offers divine pronouncements. The stalwart knight at center is our resilient ego. It faces toward Truth. By Truth's tablet of laws, the ego divides the world into four quadrants. The upper right hosts a holy angel (Truth's messenger). Three good people (the illuminated) sing in the upper left, while three bad people (the endarkened) bark in the lower right. The lower left contains a crowd of terrifying demons led by a devil to represent the untamed and terrifying unconscious. Flames motivate, ward, and guide us.

Looking at the tableau, what comes to mind? What memories does it evoke? Or consider, what meanings or stories does it inspire? You might meditate quietly on the image, perhaps with a question also in mind. Or feel free to draw your own symbolic version of this chakra.

Sometimes, people adopt a total way of perceiving and deciding. It can be any "ism." They use it to explain everything. It feels empowering and purposeful. However, that "ism" usually has them in its grip. It blinds and squeezes them, and they get highly reactive. When do you get like this?

37

4th Chakra
Balance & Intimacy

you love
you make yourself vulnerable

This is your *heart* chakra. Like a great tree, it is a place of refuge and vulnerability. You use it to commit yourself to love. When used in a balanced way, you find acceptance, harmony, and a sense of completion. The tree produces the fruit of your labors, and that fruit can create more life. Wood also shows one's character and can act as a protective shield. This chakra is home to a basic conscience: Do you heal or harm? Imbalance here invites fear of love, loneliness, neediness, and harboring of hatred, jealousy, and revenge.

The fourth chakra is *anāhata**, which means unhurt, unstruck, or unbeaten. It sits above the diaphragm around the heart and thymus gland. Though some traditions link it to the element of air, in light of Jung's analysis, it links well to the element of wood**, which represents a living, breathing union of basic material elements. As a metaphor, imagine a tree: Its roots symbolize depth, its bark shows its character, it flexes in synch with life's seasons, and it bears fruit in a healthy environment. Jung did not discuss this center directly, but we know from kundalini tradition that it is a seat of love. Therefore, unlike the other chakra descriptions, everything here draws from the wider chakra literature.

In this center, **love and commitment** replace the obsessions of the 3rd chakra, and the urge for conflict is sublimated into constructive activities. All things moderate and gain depth. Jung said, "Where love rules, there is no will to power; and where power predominates, there love is lacking. The one is the shadow of the other." We stop projecting our shadow and fighting "the other." Instead, **we start harmonizing to complement each other**. Symbolically, **the other chakra elements intersect here**: A tree requires good soil, fresh water and air, and appropriate sunlight to thrive. Similarly, the heart's four chambers symbolize a union of four elements, and when the heart gets clogged or erratic, we easily weaken or die. Interestingly, a healthy heartbeat may sound even, but when we zoom in on a heart monitor, we see numerous microscopic blips that help it quickly adapt to sudden changes. Thus, a healthy heart is both stable and adaptable. Indeed, whenever you hear someone's heartbeat and match yours to theirs, this chakra is active.

Here, we often **find peace in relationships with people who complement or "complete" us**,

* Jung linked *anāhata* to the throat and air element, which appears as the next chakra up.

4th Chakra: Balance & Intimacy
The heart is our tree of compassion for self and others, and over life's
seasons we find completeness as we stay true to love.

each person bringing strengths to cover our blind-spots. Lovedones often include a spouse, family, friends, and perhaps one's charges and mentors such as close employees, patients, or students. The more recurrent and genuine a relationship, the deeper the bond. We may mark a commitment using a ritual or object, such as a wedding ceremony or friendship ring. In daily life, this other person often complements us practically, such as fulfilling different martial duties and covering our weak points. **Psychologically, we also tend to seek those who foster in us an alchemical reaction between ego and shadow**. Jung advises, "Knowing your own darkness is the best method for dealing with the darkness of other people," and at the same time, "Everything that irritates us about others can lead us to an understanding of ourselves." For example, if we are more extraverted, rational, organized, or such, then our partner is likely more introverted, idealistic, or free-flowing, respectively. These differences, over time, will tend to bring out our shadow. Ideally, Jung says, "the meeting of two personalities is like the contact of two chemical substances: if there is any reaction, both are transformed." Unfortunately, a couple can instead end up locked into superficial roles and commitments, stuck in a life that doesn't allow them to grow or be themselves because they are too afraid to open up.

    To feed the heart, we must open up to love. This requires vulnerability, empathy, and forgiveness. Vulnerability is a willingness to express ourselves honestly, to speak in accordance with our conscience, and to feel others' joy and suffering as our own. In doing so, we may also let in poison, demons, and all sorts of agonies that can harm us, fool us, or dilute our sense of self. Moreover, as our loved-ones make deep impressions over time, they may wrong us. Such painful betrayals are a piercing wound. Though potentially dangerous, deep commitments promote growth, and love is necessarily more than adoration, like ardor of a celebrity or idol (that's the 3rd chakra). Love also requires we share a life, though once a bond forms, we can still feel connected to a person if they travel far away. Ideally, to live well with this chakra, we develop a psychological immune system to identify and neutralize the dangers.

    This chakra keeps us in touch with our humanity and conscience. Here, our identity is not categories given to us by the world. *Anāhata* doesn't care about labels. Rather, it is home to what's truly important over our lifespan. Consider what's always been keenly important to you since childhood—what defines you personally. Just as a tree's rings are a permanent history of all its years, and our immune system is an astute record-keeper of dangers, so too our loves are imprinted into our brain—written onto our heart—and will surely hold true all of our days. Moreover, because this chakra taps our great storehouse of experiences, it helps us rely on our conscience, which is a plain viscerally-felt form of consciousness. This conscience isn't reasoned or sophisticated. And instead of projecting good and evil onto others, we allow a little angel and a little devil to sit on our shoulders, understanding that we have some of both and may choose between them. With patience and honesty, we can make choices that align with our identity and commitments to keep growing slowly, like a tree.

    From this center, **we give our full loving attention to our work, which becomes our vocation rather than a "job,"** "cause," or "career" (a modern term devoid of care). In particular, this chakra helps us excel at crafting fine art, food, clothing, and other tools and items. Quality of craftsmanship

** Many traditions link the heart chakra to air but Jung did not. Wood is the next most common link.

and care of service become plainly apparent and sublime like a love of fifty years. Good literature and films also come from, and speak to, this center as genuine reflections of the human condition. Lesser pieces just pull crudely at our heart strings. Similarly, our "house" is a home kept with pride, our "yard" is a garden for delightful relaxing, and our "town" is a community of familiar faces and entertaining stories. Notice how all of these can be enjoyed in moderation, nurtured mindfully, and enjoyed in depth. Whatever sits in our hearts, the standards for respect and authenticity are very high. That said, only people—not money or goods—can truly provide a full scope of psychological engagement.

Some people close their hearts, suffer broken hearts, or form hearts of ice or stone. They may feel a metal plate is bolted onto their chest. They may be terrified to let anyone in. They may feel dizzy after a betrayal or lost loved-one. Because this chakra links to the immune system, a lack of daily love or a long-abiding despair or hatred endangers our health. A massage or purge typical of the 2nd chakra will not help. Just as love and hope abide here—springing eternal, bringing glowing color to life—so too do grief and regret, which weigh heavily on us, make life a dull gray, and depress the immune system. Our long-term defenses weaken. Then we fall into this chakra's dark side. To use a modern example, in the film *Star Wars*, Anakin Skywalker resents that his mentors keep him from his love, Padme, and also didn't let him save his mother, so he chooses revenge and transforms into Darth Vader, forever encased in a protective metal suit. Similarly, in the Bible, Judas Iscariot betrays his teacher Jesus out of greed and jealousy, then hangs himself in despair. In this center, hate and its kin—hopelessness, selfishness, and vengeance—can find a home. They occupy the heart, suffocating it and subtracting space for more revitalizing commitments. Then the heart withers, or it hardens to act as a shield against vulnerability.

Day-to-day, this chakra is more tame but no less serious, particularly when we feel insecure in ourselves and our love. We might constantly check our connection with a person, look for signals, ask for dialog, and dwell on obstacles like fear of being hurt, or of perceived resistance, or being torn between conflicting loves. Jung's advice? He said, "Your vision will become clear only when you can look into your own heart. Who looks outside, dreams; who looks inside, awakens." So follow your heart, but in practice the cultivation of deep trust and beautiful shared moments takes work.

Of all the things we might let into this chakra, the Divine is perhaps the most moving. **Do we let down our defenses and let God's light touch our hearts?** We might assume faith is anchored in the 3rd chakra, and yes, a religious person's fiery zeal may in fact come from there. However, the true home of faith is the 4th chakra. The heart can hold an internalized love of the Creator, the Source, or whatever one may call the Divine. This love is based on experience and commitment, like everything else written onto the heart. And just as deep love of a person offers *psychological* completion, so too does deep love of the Divine offer *spiritual* completion. In some cases, clergy "marry" their vocation and religious institutions, offering their whole hearts to spiritual service. But for most people, this internalized love of God simply asks that we keep reorienting ourselves to something sublime and mysterious, which is greater than ourselves and the world's glamor. It is no wonder that, in most religions, God is defined as love and as an antidote to the heart's dark times of suffering.

When we tap this center, we attend quietly to our better selves, re-orient to our core, and rededicate ourselves to our most beloved commitments. Herein lies its strengths and its weaknesses. **Imagine all the imagery of the heart.** The classic heart symbol is actually two anatomical hearts sown together, and together they may be bound with a thorny rose, pierced by a sword, skirted by angels or devils, or alight with fire. Consider the many sayings around the heart such as "love is blind," "better to have loved and lost than never to have loved at all," or Blaise Pascal's reminder, "The heart has its reasons which reason knows nothing of." Jung himself conveys the importance of love, even of knowledge: "You can know something in the head for forty years and it may never have touched the heart."

Get Loving

Here are some mindful activities with this chakra to cultivate lasting intimate relationships.

1. **Cherish your life and gifts**. Despite life's many ups and downs, you've likely done some good, helped some people, and expressed your talents in some positive ways. The downtimes and mistakes are okay too. Life is for learning. Appreciate your life's purpose and meaning and find forgiveness for your errors. This may involve reconciliation or other means of closure.

2. **Know your loved-ones**. Take stock of those you trust with your heart, that you care about deeply, and they you. These are loved-ones. Take time to listen. Get to know them, their likes and dislikes, their past and hopes for the future. Consider how they complement you and cover your flaws.

3. **Be gentle with loved-ones**. Be thoughtful in your words and deeds with your loved-ones. The Golden Rule—treating others as you want to be treated—is not sufficient because we all differ. Take time to consider what they want and need from you. Sometimes they need firm honesty.

4. **Flex your heart**. An open heart has room for infinite compassion, but do not let your care for others slip into emotional overreach. This does no service for others. Search your feelings for whether your care is pure and uncomplicated or whether it carries burdensome attachments.

5. **Practice loving kindness**. It is relatively easy to love without showing it or to love only those close to you. Practice love with strangers and "foes"—people you disagree with. Bear their attention with an open mind. Step away from negative words and actions. Communicate when you can, face-to-face with respect, or at least practice tolerance, mercy, and curiosity with others.

6. **During meditation or yoga**, focus on your heartbeat. If possible, get in touch with others' beats. Feel your heart's warmth as you visualize loved-ones. Review all the beautiful moments you've shared and kindness you've shown you to each other. Imagine opening a door or window into your chest, revealing your vulnerability. When you stand or move, lead with your chest.

7. **Give thanks each day** for God's divine love. If you wish, use another term like "the Divine", "the Source" or "the Universe." Whatever you say, when you open your heart to the Divine, you open yourself to the fruits of this chakra: deeper patience and love.

How loving are you currently? Count how much you identified above: 1   2   3   4   5   6   7

4TH CHAKRA: BALANCE & INTIMACY

Jung drew on symbols to help people get in touch with themselves and resolve their issues. You can do that too. Refer to the tableau and exercises below to explore how you use this chakra.

— Give practical care to others
— Give loving kindness to all beings
— Willing to be vulnerable
— Keep others' vulnerability safe
— Enjoy a long-term romantic coupling
— Nurture (shepherd) children, students, mentees, or similar folk
— Emotionally honest to self and others
— Treat other people as unique human beings with talents and faults like you

At center, the ego appears as two embracing hearts. Each complements the other. One is black, one is white, and each holds a small measure of the other (as a small circle) within itself. The tree's trunk and roots provide stability while branches reach into the open sky. The trunk is etched with old love notes. Fruit of love hangs from the tree. The world cycles through seasons, just as love supports and survives though life's changes. Tempting fruit on the tree in spring become a basket of edibles in summer, a harvested meal in fall, and emptiness in winter. The foundation is "LOVE."

Looking at the tableau, what comes to mind? What memories does it evoke? Or consider, what meanings or stories does it inspire? You might meditate quietly on the image, perhaps with a question also in mind. Or feel free to draw your own symbolic version of this chakra.

Select a partner, loved one, or good friend. List how he or she has contributed to your life. Be thorough. Recall specific moments. Next, do the same for how you have contributed to that person's life. Write a poem, sketch a picture, or craft a little gift. Give that person a card with your creation.

5th Chakra
Speech & Reason

you speak
you gain perspectives

> This is your *throat* chakra. Like the wind, it carries your thoughts aloud. You use it to communicate and inspire. When used in a balanced way, you easily speak your mind, listen well, express ideas through entertaining stories and clear theories, and can give or follow a line of reasoning. This chakra also offers a broad perspective just as a bird's eye view of the world lets us place ourselves and others in context. Overuse of this chakra invites chatter, gossip, indifference, lying, pointless philosophizing, rationalizing, and talk without action.

This chakra, called *vishuddha**, means "especially pure." It sits at the throat and includes the thyroid gland and the tongue and lungs to afford speech. Jung linked it to the element of air. As we breathe from this center, it lifts us up off the ground, and from our new vantage point we can look down with detachment and enjoy the benefits of objectivity and inspiration.

This center kicks off conscious psychological development. **Here, we detach and treat our ego as a "thing" to be managed** like anything else. Jung describes how we start to reason and reflect; we withdraw from our gut emotional responses to ask, "Why am I behaving like this?" and "How can I better behave myself?" These questions herald the beginning of conscious development where "the ego discovers itself as being a mere appendix of the self." At last, we step back, examine ourselves in the mirror, and are dismayed by our aimless or destructive one-sidedness. We rise to take a measured approach to our activities. We see our beliefs are poorly-informed biases and turn to experts for advice, even if doing so would feel uncomfortable. In practice, this allows us to discuss ideas we do not agree with—perhaps play devil's advocate—and work with people we dislike. The result is often a fount of ideas and options that can produce tremendous success.

In this center, the sky is the limit, talk is the main medium of communication, and nothing lasts for long. As Jung points out, **this center is more volatile than the elements of earth, water, or fire; words and reasons appear and vanish like gusts of wind**, and they gain and lose strength with suddenness and cannot be touched or pinned down. And what drives the wind? Consider how wind is generated by the heating and cooling of the air by the sun's movements, by fire. This is how, as

* Jung called this center *anāhata*, the chakra below this, but his interpretation remains useful.

5th Chakra: Speech & Reason
From lungs to throat and passing the lips, we use language to convey
feelings and knowledge, though words are as fickle as the wind.

Jung describes it, the fiery dispositions and conflicts typical of our third chakra motivate this chakra. We feel something strongly and then generate words or plans to justify or actualize those feelings. This is a reminder that behind every chakra is the hidden working of the other chakras.

With this chakra, we can say anything, mean anything, and make great leaps in reasoning. Jung compares the chakra to a gazelle. Unlike a ram for the third chakra, a gazelle is not domesticated or sacrificial. Instead, a gazelle can leap up to ten meters and is "impossible" to catch. In the same way, we can make huge leaps from observations to answers, and we can create things that move like the wind, from an actual windmill to a flurry of papers coming off a printing press. Humorously, a person stuck here might be called a "windbag." Jung points out that we can generate wind or benefit from it, but we cannot capture it in a box or transport it in a wheelbarrow. Rather, the great creations of reason and civilization move by ideas that appeal to invisible hands. This lecture reminded me of "The Wealth of Nations" (1776) by economist Adam Smith. Smith expounded on an "invisible hand" as a trusted means to power whole economies. Eventually, Jung says, **the things we cannot weigh end up having the most weight** in this center, such as "public opinion" or "the value of advertising" or the textbooks used in schools. We may even come to rely on verbal tricks: truthiness, weasel words, fitting the narrative, just-so stories, and memes about memes in order to win over others. We can be critical or inspiring here, deploying jargon and metaphors, and all of these are mere words that we can make dance in the air or blow away. Jung points to all the petals on this chakra's symbol. Each petal is inscribed with a letter of the Sanskrit alphabet, and together they describe all the possible ways of saying things.

This chakra includes **listening as well as speaking, and voice tone as well as word content**. Sometimes we get literal, such as interpreting computer code and legal contracts. Other times, for romance or in a negotiation, we focus on delivery. While words are easily manufactured and shift like the wind to mean anything, we can also weigh others' honesty and intentions as a counter-balance. Consider ways to say "I love you." Emphasize a different word as you repeat it three times. Or try a phony voice versus an authentic one. This chakra offers a lot of nuance. In kundalini, this chakra also includes poetry and kissing or "necking." Thus, sexuality often gets its start in this chakra.

Often, **we fulfill our professional vocation from this center**. We stay well-aware of the complexities of our discipline—be it counseling, construction, music, or mathematics—and we get plenty of practice sustaining a calm, competent, and pragmatic stance as we refer to the correct words and concepts for our job. Indeed, any profession that uses words or relies upon reason is raised up here. You know you are in this center when you talk or think about something with the same insight and patience that you apply in your career or other area of expertise. We know we are here when we drop pretenses, work with many variables, defer to others as needed, follow evidence and principles wherever they lead, even against our personal wishes, and craft lasting, working solutions.

Psychology is molded into a science here. The psychologist is no longer a priest or oracle, as in the 3rd chakra. Rather, the role of a clinical psychotherapist or conflict resolution specialist (note the precise wording) is to draw upon validated methodologies and best practices, such as Cognitive

Behavioral Therapy or Analytical Psychology (note how important ideas are capitalized). From a cool vantage point, the psychologist taps precise techniques to aid clients caught in the currents of the 2nd through 4th chakras; he or she may even aid others in this very chakra who are suffering from its inevitable ennui, by referencing the perspectives of the next chakra up. Whatever the specific techniques, the self-improvement can take a very long time because we've made the process rational and slowed growth down to a careful science.

Today's **"self-help" thrives as fuel to keep us working on ourselves**. Psychological instruments like a Myers-Briggs assessment seek to contain and measure the psyche with objective definitions of separate types. Ideally, these tools complement the face-to-face human interactions of a skilled facilitator and a client. But more often, one's inner life is simplified to a set of linear traits. You "take the test" and it "tells you" who you are. Then there is the kind of self-help book that debuts on shelves as a hurricane of inspirational words on how to better remodel or maximize oneself, with "new" methods, where enlightenment is a goal. In contrast, yoga is about removing things so we are free to open up like a flower. Given these cross-purposes, it is no surprise a lot of self-help falls short.*

The Western world embraced this chakra during its Age of Reason. It turned away from the 3rd chakra; crusaders became gentlemen in suits who solved problems with the pen, not in armor with swords. Thus, modern society tends to place consciousness in this dispassionate cognitive center. We no longer locate the self in the loins, diaphragm or even the heart. Instead, **consciousness is in the head and neuroscience says we are "just" bio-information processors**, akin to our favorite modern tool, the computer. If we malfunction, we can take a pill to settle down and get reprogrammed. Conversely, the body is treated as a mere vehicle, and higher chakras related to leadership, creativity, and the Divine are viewed as curiosities, only for odd or exceptional people. At the extreme, by informing us that even free will is an illusion and we must trust the certified experts to know ourselves, we are ready to be good robot-like workers, highly educated and re-educated as needed, efficient and sober, within an orderly and scientifically-managed society. At the same time, the Age of Reason has done its best to afford room for some of the better qualities of the other chakras—at least we can talk about them, even when we are out of touch with them!

Religion takes on a philosophical, principled, and/or ascetic character here. Often, an airy approach to the Divine promotes ethics and a theology that is either highly elaborate or startlingly minimalist. At the start of the Age of Reason, science-minded people like Sir Isaac Newton pursued alchemy as a blend of religion with chemistry, while others, like Thomas Jefferson, kept only the non-supernatural elements of their faith. Today, people still either dismiss abstractions like love and magic, or try to reformulate them in scientific terms, perhaps as a pseudo-science. The result is a practical distance from faith; a modern theologian might not even be religious, with religion as merely a scholarly or intellectual pursuit. Or as in Zen Buddhism and similar traditions, one aims for minimal attachments, rigorous physical and mental practices, and the cultivation of "emptiness" to become open to receiving elegant truths which, like physics equations, are beautiful in their simplicity and applicability. For these approaches, language is a powerful tool, such as framing a meditation

* *Why Spiritual Growth Does Not Lead to Enlightenment* by Christopher Wallis. http://www.tantrikstudies.org

on the question, "What is the sound of one hand clapping?"

This chakra's weakness lies in its strength. In its vortex, we are a cool skeptic of all things, yet prone to rationalizing. For example, in the 3rd chakra, the gods are often located in the sky or other unreachable places, and when we rise into the air here, in our airplanes and from our satellites, we discover no gods, or God. We scan everywhere and see no evidence for the supernatural. From an aerial vantage, **we might believe we can see, know, and manage all—if not now then eventually. But we cannot** get at what is unfelt, unheard, unseen, and inchoate. That would be like demanding color from a black-and-white photograph. At best, we fake it. To learn more, we must go to the next chakras.

Get Fluent

Here are some mindful activities with this chakra to cultivate speaking and reasoning ability.

1. **Listen objectively**. Practice stepping back to listen to yourself and others as if you were third-party observer. You may notice behavior that is defensive, aggressive, prideful, over-dramatized, glamorizing, fear-mongering, or egotistical. Evaluate news sources in the same way.
2. **Think systematically**. In every profession, people learn and apply a step-wise system such as a scientific method, legal procedure, medical test, etc. In the same way, follow processes that push consistent thinking based on evidence. Be sure to frame your conclusions as tentative and follow logically from these processes. Educate yourself on common reasoning errors.
3. **Speak effectively**. Get comfortable speaking up and communicating clearly with relevance, brevity, and honesty. This may involve face-to-face talk or outlining your points, using e-mail or recorded audio. Avoid us-versus-them language, biases (adjectives), and rationalizing ("...because...").
4. **Seek feedback**. On any project or idea, seek feedback from others. Query professionals and laypersons for a wide range of viewpoints to get the best possible outcome. Treat your own view as just one of many. Seek elegant results that balance simplicity with satisfying multiple views. Similarly, when you get upset about news or others' ideas, take a time-out to consider.
5. **Map your growth**. By this chakra, you enjoy some perspective. Articulate a system of personal enlightenment using words to accurately describe and understand your life experiences as a way to identify where you've been and where you could go. This also helps relate to others.
6. **During meditation or yoga**, focus on flexing your neck, keeping your throat clear, and chanting with clarity. Conversely, extend your periods of silence, both literally and quieting your mind's chatter. Further on, you may find yourself ready to sing, play a musical instrument, offer verbal guidance, or otherwise help others in their practice.
7. **Give thanks each day** for your education, whatever its form, particularly if provided for. Today we enjoy tremendous, globe-spanning avenues of communication and information gathering. Think of people you've met or kept in touch with. Also, give thanks for your freedom to speak.

How rational are you currently? Count how much you identified above: 1 2 3 4 5 6 7

5TH CHAKRA: SPEECH & REASON

Jung drew on symbols to help people get in touch with themselves and resolve their issues. You can do that too. Refer to the tableau and exercises below to explore how you use this chakra.

— Communicate clearly
— Persuade/inspire with honest words
— Listen patiently to what others say
— Look at situations from several views
— Define what you see and hear and follow reason to find a solution
— Create using language (stories, poetry, arguments, laws, models, etc)
— Examine yourself objectively
— Let models and data guide decisions

The outer dotted frame and perimeter of words indicate freedom to explore using language. The bird soaring above the clouds symbolizes a capacity to see the world, including ourselves, from any angle. The meter acts as a reference point. In the thought bubble, we name where we are. The couple at center speak to each other, listening with ears perked. The wavy lines are blowing wind. Heat rises from the lower chakras via a flume, which is also a throat, to generate the wind. The windmill harnesses the wind for work, while the book represents education, knowledge, and learning.

Looking at the tableau, what comes to mind? What memories does it evoke? Or consider, what meanings or stories does it inspire? You might meditate quietly on the image, perhaps with a question also in mind. Or feel free to draw your own symbolic version of this chakra.

Let's shift perspectives. First, ask a friend how he or she would likely respond in a scenario like a robbery while shopping. Listen closely. Then write a one-page vignette in the first-person view. Write as if you were that person. Get feedback and improve it. Ideally, he or she then writes for you.

6th Chakra*
Vision & Systems

you observe
you understand how it all works

This is your *third eye* chakra. It grants insight into the true workings of things. With it, you can observe the world, align yourself with a vision, and take control of your own destiny, manifesting ideas into reality. When used in a balanced way, you see through deceit, understand complex topics, solve challenges with calm ease, and organize yourself and others with integrity around a vision as a wise leader. You can juggle many resources, push past limits, and evoke respect. Imbalance invites the pride that precedes disaster.

This center, called *ājñā*, means "command," as in "a spiritual teacher's guidance." Its symbol is a winged eye, where what we see carries us to new heights. It sits between the eyes and links to the pituitary gland in our brain, which medicine calls the "master controller" of all our other glands and hormones. Traditionally in yoga, this chakra is linked to practice: building expertise, habits, and knowledge through repetition to go from darkness to light. Overall, it is our chief executive. It helps us harness and rule over the other chakras as we cultivate our higher selves.

This chakra is called our third eye. **It reflects our innate capacity to visualize in the mind something abstract, hidden, or perfect.** With it, we can imagine different places and times, the parts and movements of a machine, psychological models like chakras, our idealized selves, and concepts like justice, nature, and time. This is not like reason using words. Vision is 3D and reveals complex patterns, while voice is linear with one word at a time. Using this chakra, we can build up a working knowledge of a subject and master it. This may take years of observation, education, and practice. A guide or vision might motivate us to stick to it! However we learn, we gain expertise. A person here is like an engineer, even if he or she is an artist, chef, doctor, fashion designer, psychologist, soldier, or whatever else. In this chakra we can see, analyze or design, experiment or fix, build or demolish with professional coolness.

The myth of **the Roman goddess Minerva** fits this chakra.** Minerva's father was Jupiter, the king of the gods. We might say that, for Romans, Jupiter symbolized the highest chakra, the crown chakra, and legend says Minerva was born from Jupiter's head, making her a deity of the

---

* Jung's version of this chakra is different and starts in the next section on page 56.

6th Chakra: Vision & Systems
Using our third eye, we gain working knowledge of the world's many
invisible processes, tap life's numerous resources, and judge wisely.

mind. How did that happen? As the legend opens, Jupiter receives a prophecy that his coming child will grow strong and overthrow him, so he swallows whole Minerva's mother, Metis. Metis was known for planning, cunning, and wisdom, and she reacted. While inside Jupiter, she forged weapons and armor for their coming child, and the constant pounding gave him a headache. To relieve Jupiter's pain, the forge god Vulcan split open Jupiter's head with a hammer. From the cleft, Minerva leapt out, fully adult, wearing armor and wielding weapons. She became a goddess of knowledge and wisdom, qualities of a third eye. Specifically, she was a patron of music, poetry, medicine, commerce, weaving, crafts, and magic—the daily fruits of Roman civilization—and these fruits were not just words or ideas. They were technologies and institutions, the tangible results of using this chakra. Finally, Minerva's companion is an owl, a creature of keen sight and predatory reflexes, even in darkness. Like the owl, the third eye can see without light and swiftly find success.

As our visual center, this chakra helps us to see through deceptions, and it illuminates timeless, hidden principles. When we're solidly here, we do not act rashly or get misled by trigger words or surface appearances, much less glamor or illusions. Instead of seeing what our ego wants us to see, we just take things for what they are—as data in context. We act as a witness, like an anthropologist studying a troop of monkeys or a farmer calculating what soil to till, weeds to pull, and crops to plant. Doing this well requires we build a mental model of the world, and we keep testing and refining that model in various situations, perhaps discarding it if it fails to reflect what we see. Ideally, we also *self*-reflect to critique our own ego—*ājñā* fancies itself as chief of the chakras— and with it, we issue commands to fix ourselves rather than suffer. Earlier, in the 5th chakra, we started asking questions. Here, we can figure out answers that work.

This chakra restricts itself to the world stage. With clarity of mind, we see people as actors playing roles within plot-lines, but **we do not break "the fourth wall," which is the boundary that separates the game of life from eternity**. No matter how smart we get, the intellect by itself cannot see beyond *māyā*, which names the world as a distraction from an unfathomable divine plan. That's why it is easy to mistake the 3rd chakra, the solar plexus, for this one. In that chakra, a person thinks he is smart and sees "the Truth," but his ego deludes him. The tip-offs are many. For example, he goes on an us-versus-them crusade rather than striving with calm curiosity for a win-win solution. He mistakes a confident ego for maturity. Learning the world's many ins-and-outs takes time.

This chakra often manifests as a drive to exert control over ourselves and the world through an efficient, strategic use of tools. Humans are tool users and tool makers. Anything can be a tool, even the ego. This center is like a forge, a set of armaments, a machine shop, an iron throne, or a skyscraper. It is a fortress against failure and a ward against empty words. If this chakra had a physical element, it would be metal—strong and efficient with many uses, but brittle. By the time we reach this chakra, we've lived long enough to know success takes a constant balancing of qualities, just as a bird flies by constantly balancing its wings. Crafting takes effort and flow, drive and patience, cooperation and vigilance, skepticism and faith, and elegance and complexity. It is not "either/or." It is "both/ and." Maybe we aim to build a shining city on a hill, harness wild horses, or awaken and align all of our chakras. Whatever the aim, this chakra gives us the genius and mental stamina to do so.

** Minerva, Jupiter, and Vulcan are Athena, Zeus, and Hephaestus in Greek mythology.

This chakra is our seat of higher conscience, also called integrity or wisdom. With this center's aid, you can manifest your best self and your best life, a harmonious life where you act responsibly—not by acting out big, dramatic productions, but by being a calm and curious adult. In the Biblical story of the wise King Solomon, two women came for advice. Both claimed an infant son as her own. Who was the true mother? Solomon had to decide. He looked past the obvious choices. He proposed bisecting the baby, and each woman would get half. The first woman agreed, while the second preferred that the first woman get the baby rather than kill him. Their answers illuminated the truth, and Solomon awarded the boy to the second woman. This response differs from the heart chakra, *anāhata*, which simply offers an obvious angel and devil on each shoulder. Using this chakra, we draw out our own and others' inner guidance systems because we strive for right action. Those few who master this center bring truth and justice as they help others understand the deeper meanings of the situations in their lives. Conversely, those who misuse or shut off this center are deceitful, power-hungry, and egotistical exploiters, manipulators, and tyrants. They even blind themselves to their own lies.

How can we tap this chakra smartly? It sits just above our current societal norm, which is the 5th chakra. Thus, this chakra is an aspiration. Using it well takes searching and effort, where each person must forge his or her own way. Historically, people saw church and university as high-minded visions of character and intellect. Today, **we may manifest this chakra by cultivating professionalism in our careers.** Many careers task us with complexity—think of engineering, governance, and medicine. In the previous airy throat chakra, *vishuddha*, we took different perspectives and wove ideas from words. But that was just talk and raw data. Here, we must apply our words and face consequences. Can we walk the talk? Can we translate knowledge into success? For example, a young doctor might get by on school knowledge and what companies and colleagues tell him. Alternatively, like the brilliant detective Sherlock Holmes, he learns to view each patient as a big puzzle that is complicated but solvable. He gathers and considers many facts and factors, and he understands how lifestyle, genes, attitude, and medicine all interact with body, heart, and mind to help each patient personally.

Psychologically speaking, when we reach this chakra, **we aim to transcend the limitations of the human ego and become like little gods on this planet.** Everywhere today we may see this chakra's fruits and its pitfalls. Over the long span of history, our best minds have applied themselves to many problems, resulting in wondrous boons. Compared to beasts, we are now little gods. One of the greatest boons, alongside hot food and pleasant shelter, is the power of modern medicine—notably surgery and antibiotics. We take drugs to deal with lack of sleep, pain, impotence, dangerous pregnancies, and many bodily ills. We no longer need to feel weak. Our egos no longer feel insulted. We suffer less of Nature's fates, and our destiny seems more in our own hands. We can be little monarchs, wise or tyrannical. Many of these boons are masks for the greatest challenge to our egos: mortality. After all, gods do not die, do they? In recorded history, medicine has dramatically increased the length and quality of mortality from pre-birth through old age. Of all modern professions, although we might think of the engineer, industrialist, general, artiste or humanitarian, the ultimate expression of this chakra is the medical doctor who presides over life and death.

Our bright future—a product of keen minds—looms on the horizon. Will the future result from wise intellects, from pride that precedes disaster, or a mix of both? We are close to living in a world when we can guide our own genetics, employ robotic slaves, and merge with machines to expand consciousness. In the past, complex societies like the Roman Empire have collapsed. Can we turn fate to destiny? Might we design intelligent machines that will design more intelligent machines to manage us? Remember King Solomon. He asked for and received wisdom from God, but he became complacent from success, then decadent and foolish. Even King Solomon fell against the powerful urges of his psyche, his unconscious. This takes us to the next section, to Jung's version of this chakra.

Get Integral

Here are some mindful activities with this chakra to cultivate integrity, professionalism, and wisdom.

1. **Create your future.** Think of the life you really want to enjoy each day and what accomplishments of service you wish to leave for the world. Then brainstorm and figure out ways to take control of your future to make that future happen.

2. **Replace bad habits.** Examine how you think, where you place your attention, and your response patterns. Be honest with yourself. What works for you? What is just bias, stories, and fake drama? Go through each of the chakras from bottom to top, locate the negative manifestations, and release them to make room for the gifts and good habits each of them brings.

3. **Cultivate nobility.** This means being noble in character, mind, and perhaps earned rank. It includes qualities such as decency, goodness, honor, integrity, and virtue. Consider what nobility looks like for you. Visualize that and find ways to manifest it in your life. Become your best self.

4. **Get integral.** Whenever you have an idea or endeavor, consider how to make it whole and complete. For example, when tending your outdoor garden, consider how choices and changes will impact the whole system. Similarly for any value or goal, act with integrity. For example, as the saying goes, charity begins at home. The result of "integral action" is harmony.

5. **Build something.** Go through the process of crafting something of quality. Apply your mental muscles to make it the best it can be. Learn the relevant tools, materials, and techniques. Apply as much focus and discipline as you can muster. Accept and deal with mistakes. You may surprise yourself!

6. **During meditation or yoga**, focus your gaze inward. Allow thoughts to freely come and go, without dwelling on them. Observe your busy mind as you would observe a busy crowd of strangers. What do you see? Grant space for any kind of person. Then let an image of yourself rise in your mind's eye. What is beautiful about this person? Keep guiding yourself back to that beauty.

7. **Give thanks each day** for the blessings of civilization and the fruits of turning reason into reality: agriculture, education, industry, philosophy, science, and technology. Acknowledge people who make all this possible. Dedicate yourself to contribute in similar constructive endeavors.

How integral are you currently? Count how much you identified above: 1 2 3 4 5 6 7

6A CHAKRA: VISION & SYSTEMS

Jung drew on symbols to help people get in touch with themselves and resolve their issues. You can do that too. Refer to the tableau and exercises below to explore how you use this chakra.

— Act with integrity
— Actively unmask illusions and deceptions (i.e. "follow the money")
— Test yourself to stay humble
— Stay tuned-in to your conscience
— Think systems, not just intentions: inputs, processes, and consequences
— Master your tools like a professional
— Seek win-win solutions
— Lead across conflicting groups

The psyche is a three-eyed monarch. The ego has built itself into an idol, cyborg, superhero, or such. The right hand sports money. The coin safely contains one's *anima* (or *animus* if female). The left hand sports a tesseract, symbolizing complexity. The third eye sits as a crown that grants wisdom, a will to create the future, and a deep working understanding of the world. The city, satallite in orbit, and globe stand for one's self and the world as a system. The owl lets us see and strike even in darkness. The throne of prosperity is our reward for integrity. The outer frame is a placeholder for the current era.

Looking at the tableau, what comes to mind? What memories does it evoke? Or consider, what meanings or stories does it inspire? You might meditate quietly on the image, perhaps with a question also in mind. Or feel free to draw your own symbolic version of this chakra.

Pick a topic to grok more deeply. Educate yourself about it. As you learn, list all the factors (variables) related to it. Note how they influence each other. Then draw a network with the factors as circles and the influencers as arrows ("+" is promote, "-" is inhibit). Locate the most influential factors.

Jung's 6th Chakra
Psyche & Imagination

you dream
you learn from the unconscious

> This is your *inward third eye* chakra. Like a dream, it is anywhere yet nowhere and, like outer-space, it offers a total view of the world. You use it to contemplate what only the mind's eye can see, such as alternate realities. When used in a balanced way, you deal in ambiguity, are creative and imaginative, and can easily shift yourself and influence others, perhaps without their awareness. You might understand any viewpoint and merge opposites into new ideas. Overuse here invites absurdity, confusion, harebrained schemes, and madness.

This center, often called *ājñā*, means "perceive" or "beyond wisdom" in Sanskrit. Healthy use grants us imagination, insight, inspiration, and intuition. It links to the void element, also called *ether*, and perhaps sits at the back of the head. When we heed it, we learn, and when caught in its vortex, we live a purely "psychical" existence as Jung says, where *everything* pertains to the psyche. It is a starry realm of possibilities, dreams, prophecies, and imagination that we can only visit wearing a "spacesuit," as it provides no air or nutrients for us to thrive as material beings.

This chakra is a strange place. Jung describes how it penetrates through all existence. It is everywhere but cannot be felt or measured. **It is an ever-shifting polychromatic land of archetypes, shadow selves, complexes, and other psychological entities that take on forms and meanings but are never solid.** When we look into the mirrors of the mind, we may see ourselves as old, as a child, as a rabbit, as a future president, or now as in an alternate reality entirely. Jung explains, "whatever happens is truly your own subjective experience." It is the ultimate virtual reality space, where "you" are a minor player, nothing is as it seems, and everything is relative and possible. Although this psychic realm sounds very sophisticated, we visit it all the time when play-acting, especially as children. For an adult in this chakra, Jung says, "the material world is only the skin on a balloon where the psychical reality is within." And within, we do not need to justify anything based on other chakras—material existence, reason, feelings, events, measures or such. Rather, everything is "merely" a psychological dynamic or projection.

Everything takes on multiple meanings here, and all meanings are partially true *and* false.

* Jung called this center *vishuddha*, a chakra below this, but his interpretation remains useful.

Jung's 6th Chakra: Psyche & Imagination
We tap strange imagery from the unconscious, get in touch with the
many archetypes, and perform alchemy for spiritual growth.

We can conceive of the chakras themselves in many ways: literal, metaphorical, and/or otherwise—in contrast to the 2nd chakra, which defines them by sensation; the 3rd chakra, which admits only what's holy or profane; or the 5th chakra, which demands a rational view. With its rich diversity and paradoxes, this chakra is a well-spring for flexible thought and imagination. It is home to mythic elements like the *Oedipus* complex and Hero's Journey. Consider images like "a knight in shining armor," "earth mother," or "Jesus on the cross." These are symbols with multiple abstract interpretations. They are wells that we can keep returning to. Alas, this chakra lacks the means to express itself in a safe, practical, and coherent way in the material world. Thus, it is kindling for creativity and growth filtered by the other chakras.

These days, we tend to revere yet fear this center. Jung says, **from our contemporary vantage point, we see it but we do not trust a purely psychological existence; we must still attend to a material world**, and we speak of it with hesitation or frame it as a servant of a more grounded chakra. For example, psychologists might say "personality analysis is a tool" that "boosts employee retention," and we tend to limit ourselves to the results of validated instruments and authoritative scholarship rather than get into "woo-woo." This is understandable. Yes, the psychic realm is abstract. But Jung goes further: Psyche is a self-moving thing "within us" and "around us," and this chakra hosts the psychological-made-real through experience—beyond reason and words. It results from our collective human inheritance and a multitude of lived events and, within its murky, Escher-like architecture, it acts as a repository of wisdom—a wisdom that never sports a singularly clear meaning. Due to the psyche's inchoate nature, Jung says we "resist and complain" about visiting here, and we only do so with aids when tasked to, and then we return back to earth to our regular lives. Thus, we might attend a self-help seminar or an acting or writing workshop, delve into a character or three, gain some insight, then return home to deal with practical tasks of bills and kids, letting our explorations fade into the background.

Happily, **Jung bequeathed us the means to explore this chakra, both as individuals and as a society**. He developed a language to view and talk about this chakra based on a wealth of wide-ranging cross-cultural research and hands-on work with clients. He also developed techniques like active imagination to access and leverage the psychical space. In fact, psychological type historian Peter Geyer asserts that Jung did not intend for his work to be a formal, defined model of the psyche. Rather, Jung offered a therapeutic framework that relies on symbols to act as a bridge into this chakra. If his work were precisely defined, it would be mechanical, limited, and dry. This is likely why Jung's work resists attempts by naysayers, because it acts an effective spaceship to visit a realm we dream of but where we cannot normally dwell.

Jung says the **visions erupting from the psyche are usually of a non-personal nature**. He said, "The personal side is really perfectly negligible," and "they are experiences which really mean the development of Kundalini and not of Mrs. So-and-So." Regarding a female client's dreams, he explained, "A very clever analyst would be able to analyze out of that material a series of personal incidents in her life, but it would be from... our rational point of view of this world as the definite world." For example, during meditation, you might suffer a vision of a man ready to commit suicide. Jung counsels that it is symbolic of impending change or a lesson on empathy. Or, more broadly, consider activities like tarot readings and astrology. Determining personal meanings from these speaks to this chakra—we're psychonauts using otherworldly tools—but rarely do they give satisfying answers or impact behavior. In fact, we might regret going down these rabbit holes. Why? Jung points out how psychical reality is still "opposed by material reality"; we have animal bodies, require food and shelter, and so forth. Or we might dream of being the opposite sex, but that's not a call for an actual sex change. "Our conscious experience is but an appendage" of the psychological realm, a subset with many shadowy rooms, so we are easily lost. We may wonder what happens when a whole group or society gets caught in this chakra's vortex.

In this center, **there is no "correct" model of the world, only ideas of how it might be, and the power of our imagination to motivate change, akin to the placebo effect.** Consider the fantastical satire, *Alice in Wonderland*. Now imagine it is being read by an android at a Disney-like theme park in the android's off time while it is set to "dreaming" mode, and all of this is portrayed in a science fiction TV show. What precisely *is* real? Nothing, actually? And yet these stories often speak to us. They may inspire, repel, or confuse us. If we ask the android if he's conscious, he may even say "yes!" And if we act on this, it may impact reality, although how is never sure or clear. Self-development here is equally tricky. When we delve into the shadow realms of our psyche, far beyond the ego, what is and is not us is a bog, and there is no correct way to assess or develop who we are.

Rarely, a person "masters" the psychical life. Jung tapped this space consciously to benefit his own growth, and for his patients, colleagues, and the world after his time. Similarly, the Father of Hypnosis, Milton Erickston, wove metaphorical stories to bypass people's ego defenses, to speak directly to his patients' unconscious minds. Often his stories would contain their own stories, like a set of nested Russian dolls. His techniques worked even when people were not formally hypnotized! In fact, hypnosis is a potent tool to explore this realm, particularly when we hold an intention, speak in its tentative language of "maybe" and "you might," and think in terms of archetypes: virgins, dragons, knights, and such. Whatever the means and goals, mastering this chakra requires experience, intuition, a talent for metaphor, tolerance for uncertainty, a rejection of the "known," and a sense of humor. Living here is like learning how to engage in lucid dreaming: when you are asleep and yet also conscious that you are having a dream, and you can begin to conduct the dream life.

On a cultural scale, **a master of *ājñā* can craft symbols and slogans that move organizations, groups, generations, and nations.** Through the use of props, clothing, words, gestures, and such, a master can repackage a politician into an archetypal form such as "kindly grandmother" or "powerful warrior" and weave narratives around that visage; this is most effective when a culture's underlying currents already flow in that direction, such as a nation in need of healing or revenge after suffering defeat in war. Just prior to World War II, Jung spoke about the imagery of the Nazis as paralleling the German people's old pagan god Wotan. Less darkly, organizations engage in branding, and corporate leaders with charisma and vision can use imagination to project an image outward onto the canvas of the world to influence others and craft idols and shibboleths that influence the lower chakras. Alternatively, for spiritual purposes, religious texts such as the Bible's rich narration of history speaks to people for millennia precisely because of their multi-faceted psychological meanings.

Just as we may play within immersive video game worlds today, **it is plausible that our technology will someday become so advanced and our comfort with diversity so great that we can manifest the psychical life in a variety of real or nearly-real ways.** You might become the princess or the dragon or whatever you wish. We all will live in a land of a million Hindu gods. Perhaps such a world can exist when all material needs are met by machines and there is no "work" like we know today. Most work will be psychological. Does this prospect excite you? Are you really ready to float free in a void where everything is something else—and nothing?

Get Creative
Here are some mindful activities with this chakra to cultivate imagination and growth.

1. **Inspire growth**. Attend workshops and retreats; gather inspirational images, quotations, or totems; read or journal, or do meditations or prayers to inspire different parts of yourself. Travel and a change of cultures can evoke the imagination. Surround yourself with people who do the same.
2. **Engage in creative projects**. Everyone is creative, although we do not always have the time, hear the call, or even consider what we do as "creative." Whether you try painting, playing music, playing games, home remodeling, sewing or knitting, scrapbooking or such, just do it without setting standards. Treat it as a fun hobby to explore.
3. **Look for patterns**. Take in books and films, noting similarities and differences. Similarly, study biographies, histories, institutions, cultures, conversations, and innovations, open to noticing patterns. Patterns might be narrative, cyclical, multi-dimensional, quantum, chaotic or whatever.
4. **Explore altered states**. Mind the different states you experience daily—from half-asleep daydreaming to peak-performance creative flow—and find ways to leverage these. Not all are healthy or useful. Also, learn about states such as hypnosis, lucid dreaming, meditative trance, or psychedelics. Explore with intention for the purpose of discovery. Take notes.
5. **Integrate polarities**. Notice when you're pulled in different directions by conflicting parts of yourself. Some parts are quiet or angry. Learn to evoke these parts through imagination, dreamwork or such. Hear from each part and find ways to reconcile their needs. This is an alchemical process.
6. **During meditation or yoga**, focus on visualizing or communing with the archetypes. Pose questions to yourself and blank your mind, making room to invite the "little gods" (of the psyche) to appear and answer in whatever form. With them, explore questions of past and future, but be careful. This exercise is just to think imaginatively outside your box, and is not reality at all.
7. **Give thanks each day** to your life's teachers. Consider any spiritual guides or conceptual tools like the chakras framework. Include your unconscious, which is home to all the parts of you that generate your creativity and help you grow. Ask yourself what you created or learned every day.

How creative are you currently? Count how much you identified above: 1   2   3   4   5   6   7

6B CHAKRA: PSYCHE & IMAGINATION

Jung drew on symbols to help people get in touch with themselves and resolve their issues. You can do that too. Refer to the tableau and exercises below to explore how you use this chakra.

— Expand your horizons with travel and workshops, for lifelong learning
— Engage in creative projects
— Attend to psychological patterns/ habits in yourself and others
— Explore altered states of conscious-ness and journal those experiences
— Integrate opposing forces, motives, and values within yourself
— Explore some healthy alter egos

The dotted frame means open boundaries. Within, psychedelic images from the unconscious run riot. The alien couple represent *anima* and *animus*, the hidden archetypical man or woman within us that aids growth. They stand within a flowering lotus, which symbolizes the flow of kundalini en-ergy. The snake and moon are female archetypes. The cactus and rocket are male ones. The breathless stars are yet more psychical elements. The eye stands for lucid dreaming. The mirror means self-reflec-tion. There is no sun. After all, this is the unconscious. Instead, a luminous crystal presides above it all.

Looking at the tableau, what comes to mind? What memories does it evoke? Or consider, what meanings or stories does it inspire? You might meditate quietly on the image, perhaps with a question also in mind. Or feel free to draw your own symbolic version of this chakra.

You can get more in touch with your psyche's hidden landscape. First, name your top three films or novels. Next, summarize them in a paragraph, as if talking to a child. Focus on what you liked most. Then, locate the themes they share. Those are likely your unconscious life themes.

7th Chakra
Unity & Awakening

you evolve
you connect back to the Divine

This is your *crown* chakra. Like divine light, it reconnects you to the unifying source of all things. You use it to quiet your ego, grow spiritually, and find your purpose in life. When used in a balanced way, you enjoy peace amid chaos, resolve paradoxes (like "detached compassion") and easily see through the world's distractions. This chakra is also a means to altered states of consciousness and supernatural experiences. Under-use invites lack of purpose, wandering in darkness, and wasted efforts in the false light of life's mirage.

The ultimate chakra, *sahasrāra*, sits above the crown of your head and is depicted as a lotus of one thousand petals. This chakra's element is light. Within its luminous realm, there is no physical reality, suffocating baggage, passionate desires, beloved attachments, detached reason, or psychodynamics. These all vanish like colored light going back through a prism to re-merge into white again. Jung says, "there is nothing apart from or against us" here. In short, this chakra is a fully conscious experience, full of wisdom and entirely free of conflicts.

Psychologically speaking, Jung explains that the person who was but a seed in the 1st chakra is **"now in the full blazing white light, fully conscious.** In other words, the God that has been dormant in *mūlādhāra* is here fully awake, the only reality." Even in the previous chakra, *ājñā*, psychological reality was still opposed by material reality, but not here. This chakra space lies in another (higher) dimension, where "you" are an astral self beyond space and time, emotion and reason, history and identity. You are "one with the psychological realm rather than an appendage of it." Jung says this space is "**the center of the *unio mystica*** with the power of God, meaning that absolute reality where one is nothing but psychic reality, yet confronted with the psychic reality that one is not. And that is God. **God is the eternal psychical object.**"

Where can you buy a travel ticket to this astonishing destination? Indeed, how often are any of us here? **Lucky and experienced yoga practitioners will recognize Jung's words from firsthand experience**: It comes as an actual expanse of clear white light where "you" are fully present as a conscious being yet without the weight of "your" life. Indeed, you feel no attachments at all, and because

* Jung called this center *ājñā*, the chakra below this one, but his interpretation remains useful.

7th Chakra: Unity & Awakening
When we activate our kundalini energy, chakras open and align,
boundaries and polarities vanish, and ego merges with the cosmos.

there is nothing to protect, compassion and clarity reign as "you" perceive, communicate, understand, and otherwise have experiences. Besides yoga, other means such as Holotropic Breathwork and entheogens (indigenous shamanic medicines) can activate this center. This chakra, like the others, is part of our natural human endowment, though it is likely the least active, particularly in a modern world of media stimulus and endless to-do lists of practical, rational activities. Ironically, the best ways today to activate this chakra are "primitive" or pre-modern, such as yoga or shamanism. And it seems that anyone, under extreme duress or in the wee hours of the morning, may visit here.

This chakra invokes a nondual state, where ego vanishes. In the words of Martin Ball, a religion professor and author on entheogens, the ego is an "illusory energetic construct." It is "a collection of limited energetic patterns that are utilized by individuals across all levels of their being to create a sense of self and personal identity: tone of voice, body language, thought patterns, belief systems, gestures, etc. What the full nondual experience reveals is that these are simply constructs, and there is no essential individual self beyond these patterns that are continually engaged to maintain the ongoing fiction of the self as a particular identity. What lies beyond the artifice of identity is nondual universal consciousness that transcends the divides of subject and object, self and other." Happily, certain practices and substances "relax these limited energetic patterns and habits of the ego, allowing individuals to experience their true universal nature."

Activating this chakra requires extra work because it involves the other chakras. Even the indigenous shamanic medicines tend to be physically taxing, often purgative, and demand self-reflection. This is not a surprise. Jung says, "Suppose somebody reached [this chakra], the state of complete consciousness, not only self-consciousness. That would be an exceedingly extended consciousness which includes everything—energy itself.... In such an extended consciousness all the chakras would be simultaneously experienced, because it is the highest state of consciousness, and it would not be the highest if it did not include all the former experiences."

Whatever the work, it sounds worthwhile. **Some practitioners describe a gradual transition to a blissful state while others describe an abrupt episode of intense anxiety or even a frightening death as the ego fights against surrender**. But this is a mere bump. The person blanks out and reappears in the clear white light, where timeless experience is beyond words. Importantly, as one returns and re-dons his or her fictive life clothing, there are opportunities to re-examine and discard burdening and intractable life choices. As the 13th century poet Rumi says of the world, "This place is a dream. Only a sleeper considers it real. Then death comes like dawn, and you wake up laughing at what you thought was your grief." Jung might have referenced Jesus Christ's death on the cross, descent into the underworld, and glorious return to life. As art portrays, those who make the journey return with a luminous halo as their crown.

It is difficult to say whether what's gained is "for real" from these transcendent experiences. Can one gain "true" insights into the cosmic machine, akin to conversations with God? Or is any interpretation merely crafted by the ego after the fact to fill up emptiness created by the experience? Whatever the case, **people return changed, often subtly but significantly reset to a new normal.**

Subjective experience shifts with behavior. The result is often paradoxical. One may feel great joy yet also detached from life's distractions, or one may gain intense clarity of purpose while feeling "empty," free of armaments, blinders, labels, and habits. In particular, various bio-psycho-spiritual methods are gaining traction today to tap this chakra and help free people from addiction, anxiety, depression, post-traumatic stress disorder, and other ills. Peer-reviewed studies are showing efficacy that surpasses drugs, often by a wide margin. In all cases, patients' views of themselves and others, Nature and the Divine, also change. It is not like taking a pill. Jung explains, "When you succeed in the awakening of the Kundalini, so that [the energy coil] begins to move out of [its] mere potentiality, you necessarily start a world which is a world of eternity, totally different from our world." There is lasting impact—a transformation—for the whole person.

Visiting this chakra can result in a "spiritual emergency" as coined by transpersonal psychologist Stanislav Grof. This happens when a person suffers a crisis of identity and becomes unsure of what's real or meaningful. After all, what is the point of working or even living when the world is an illusion? Some people experience profound peace, joy, liberation, and connection when the veil of the world lifts, when assumptions and limitations—our containers and labels—melt away. In contrast, others feel ungrounded, alone, and adrift in a sea of new, intense emotions, unusual thoughts, rash urges, and shifts in perception. It is not psychosis. It is spiritual shock. Thus, the common advice after visiting this chakra is that the bigger its impact, the longer one should wait before implementing a significant life change.

If we are fortunate enough to benefit from this chakra, how can we keep its gifts with us in daily life? Jung says that **time spent in any chakra "is really a continuous development**. It is not leaping up and down, **for what you have arrived at is never lost.**" Even when you think you have visited somewhere and returned home, "it is an illusion that you return—you have left something of yourself in the unconscious." He continues, "If you have really experienced it, you cannot lose this experience." Jung mentions the ancient gods Wotan and Osiris and refers to author Jakob Boehme, who wrote a book about a "reversed eye" after he was "enchanted into the center of nature." In the book, "one of his eyes was turned inward; it kept on looking into the underworld—which amounts to the loss of one eye. He had no longer two eyes for this world. So when you have actually entered a higher chakra you never really turn back; you remain there."

People who cultivate this chakra tend to shift their views of spirituality and the Divine. Religious traditions tend to say we take what we've learned in life into the afterlife. Perhaps there, we may exist in this chakra, or something similar, and depending upon one's beliefs, we remain for a spell there before returning or we remain for eternity (in *sahasrāra*, those two outcomes are the same). In 1959, Dr. Jung appeared in a BBC television interview. When asked if he believed in God, he replied, "I don't need to believe, I know." As he explained elsewhere, his path to this answer came out of his experience, knowledge, and reasoning as a psychiatrist and researcher. In light of his extraordinary insights and symbology in *The Red Book** with its serpents, rushes of fiery energy, and similar imagery, there's a decent chance he had a strong personal experience in this chakra.

Some people say this chakra helps us access a timeless **cosmic consciousness, "a higher**

* *The Red Book: A Reader's Edition* by C. G. Jung, Sonu Shamdasani, Editor. W. W. Norton & Co., 2012.

form of consciousness than that possessed by the ordinary man."* Philosopher and psychologist William James defined "cosmic consciousness" as a collective consciousness, **a "larger reservoir of consciousness,"** which manifests itself within individuals and remains intact after the dissolution of the individual. It may "retain traces of the life history of its individual emanation." Working from this definition, mystics speak of psychic powers, access to records of the past or precognitive access to the future, and the existence of alien-like beings and "ascended masters" who have shed their earthly bodies and continue on in spirit form. This view proposes that humanity as a whole race may one day ascend to this higher condition.

Get Awakened

Here are some mindful activities with this chakra to cultivate a life of compassion and wisdom.

1. **Engage in a spiritual practice**. A practice is something you do. It often requires sacrifices as you "wake up" to the Divine. A practice can be comforting, and also unpleasant and humbling. It may be unsafe and negate worldly success. Whatever the practice, keep at it with courage and trust, even when you falter or take breaks.
2. **Stay awake**. Our senses and society tell us that worldly concerns are what matter. But consider, like in the film, *The Matrix*, the world is possibly a simulation. Maybe consciousness is all there is, and though there appears to be separation, what if all is one? To stay awake, act as though the world is a comprehensive illusion where we (everyone) only interacts with the shadow of things.
3. **Renounce worldly distractions**. Strive to take off all the masks, filters, and blinders. Be practical by being present in the moment—not living in the future, past, or according to games, desires, or affections. Eschew the world's labels, categories, and false identifiers. Practice quieting the ego.
4. **Stay responsible**. Your time and resources in this life are limited, so focus on your life's core obligations (such as family) and on your mission and life purpose (such as your vocation). Only put effort into people and activities that align with these responsibilities. Pass on all the rest.
5. **Act as a spiritual guide**. The greatest responsibility is the spiritual care of others. Growing into this role will likely take years as you engage in the practices that fit your journey, whether as a guide, guru, priest, psychologist, shaman, or other similar role.
6. **During meditation or yoga**, practice extending and deepening your experience of divine light. Moreover, look for ways to call it forth regularly during everyday waking life such that you become the calm in the eye of any storm, standing and moving with detached compassion and curious indifference, to be "a part of the world but not of it."
7. **Give thanks each day** for the gift and mystery of your very existence. Give thanks for the many opportunities to learn and grow, even when painful. And give thanks to all other souls who've struggled to leave the world a better place. Gratitude grants peace in the eye of life's storms.

How awakened are you currently? Count how much you identified above: 1   2   3   4   5   6   7

* *Cosmic Consciousness: A Study in the Evolution of the Human Mind* by Richard M. Bucke. Merchant Books, 2015.

7TH CHAKRA: UNITY & AWAKENING

Jung drew on symbols to help people get in touch with themselves and resolve their issues. You can do that too. Refer to the tableau and exercises below to explore how you use this chakra.

— Acknowledge your spiritual need
— Seek a "kundalini awakening" or similar direct experience of the Divine
— Follow daily practices to stay "awake"
— Renounce worldly distractions, false identifications, and harmful habits
— Focus on your core life mission
— Be fully present with a quiet mind
— Open and align all the other chakras
— Act as a spiritual guide

The frame is manifold, faint, and dotted. We float within the Divine, reeturning to our Source. The multiple frames are shifts in reality. We and existence are vibrating. The curtain that normally separates the world and divine mystery is parted, at least for a time. There is no single ego, only conscious awareness indicated by the large eye at the top, which crowns the circles below it. Those circles are the chakras. The intertwining circular and radiating lines are freely flowing streams of kundalini energy. They also stand for physical and psychological energy fields. They are in constant motion.

Looking at the tableau, what comes to mind? What memories does it evoke? Or consider, what meanings or stories does it inspire? You might meditate quietly on the image, perhaps with a question also in mind. Or feel free to draw your own symbolic version of this chakra.

For most people, activating this chakra is the main challenge. For those with an awakening experience, integrating its lessons into everyday life is their calling. When people talk about a "higher self," that's more than an ideal space or a goal. It is like an elevator. What is your daily "elevator"?

Chakra Snapshots

1st Chakra (Root): *Soil & Seed*

This is your *root* chakra. Like the earth, it lends support. You use it to stay grounded in your body and to meet your basic material needs. When used in a balanced way, you stay in synch with your physical environment, find comfort in the familiar, and enjoy a secure place you can call home. This chakra also links to cultural norms, attention to factual practicalities, and the blueprint of your potential. Overuse of this chakra invites materialism, lack of self-awareness, and disinterest in change beyond day-to-day activities.

2nd Chakra (Sacral): *Danger & Renewal*

This is your *sacral* chakra. Like water, it is essential for growth. You use it to stay connected to yourself and to others through shared experiences. When used in a balanced way, you keep up good health habits, stay in touch with your body cycles and emotional responses, and easily enjoy others' company, including close contact. Water also prompts adventures, spurs your potential through reflection, and is a place of renewal. Imbalance invites disconnection, low self-esteem, and ill health from pent-up stress, hurt, and anger.

3rd Chakra (Solar Plexus): *Action & Projection*

This is your *solar plexus* chakra. Like a fire, it sets you alight with idealism. You use it to energetically advance an empowering truth, mission, or cause. When used in a balanced way, you stand tall with confidence, know your values and beliefs, and easily stay brave and strong to advance your calling or goals. Fire also warms and illuminates, burns away all that's rubbish, and is a sign of civilization. Overuse of this chakra invites fanaticism, mythologizing of people and objects into angels and demons, and blindness to one's own faults.

4th Chakra (Heart): *Balance & Empathy*

This is your *heart* chakra. Like a great tree, it is a place of refuge and vulnerability. You use it to commit yourself to love. When used in a balanced way, you find acceptance, harmony, and a sense of completion. The tree produces the fruit of your labors, and that fruit can create more life. Wood also shows one's character and can act as a protective shield. This chakra is home to a basic conscience: Do you heal or harm? Imbalance here invites fear of love, loneliness, neediness, and harboring of hatred, jealousy, and revenge.

What's This? The snapshots below provide a quick reference to the chakras. The next four pages present a set of symbolic diagrams or *tableaus* that explain the chakras visually as Jung explained them.

5th Chakra (Throat): *Speech & Reason*

This is your *throat* chakra. Like the wind, it carries your thoughts aloud. You use it to communicate and inspire. When used in a balanced way, you easily speak your mind, listen well, express ideas through entertaining stories and clear theories, and can give or follow a line of reasoning. This chakra also offers a broad perspective just as a bird's-eye view of the world lets us place ourselves and others in context. Overuse of this chakra invites chatter, gossip, indifference, lying, pointless philosophizing, rationalizing, and talk without action.

6th Chakra (Third Eye): *Vision & Systems*

This is your *third eye* chakra. It grants insight into the true workings of things. With it, you can observe the world, align yourself with a vision, and take control of your own destiny, manifesting ideas into reality. When used in a balanced way, you see through deceit, understand complex topics, solve challenges with calm ease, and organize yourself and others with integrity around a vision as a wise leader. You can juggle many resources, push past limits, and evoke respect. Imbalance invites the pride that precedes disaster.

Jung's 6th Chakra (Third Eye): *Psyche & Imagination*

This is your *inward third eye* chakra. Like a dream, it is anywhere yet nowhere and, like outer space, it offers a total view of the world. You use it to contemplate what only the mind's eye can see, such as alternate realities. When used in a balanced way, you deal in ambiguity, are creative and imaginative, and can easily shift yourself and influence others, perhaps without their awareness. You might understand any viewpoint and merge opposites into new ideas. Overuse here invites absurdity, confusion, harebrained schemes, and madness.

7th Chakra (Crown): *Unity & Awakening*

This is your *crown* chakra. Like divine light, it reconnects you to the unifying source of all things. You use it to quiet your ego, grow spiritually, and find your purpose in life. When used in a balanced way, you enjoy peace amid chaos, resolve paradoxes (like "detached compassion"), and easily see through the world's distractions. This chakra is also a means to altered states of consciousness and supernatural experiences. Underuse invites lack of purpose, wandering in darkness, and wasted efforts in the false light of life's mirage.

1ST CHAKRA

The outer frame is the whole material world and one's culture. Within, the circle stands for female wholeness while the tiered pyramid stands for male hierarchy. The main cavity is a cave, ovum, or womb with cords or roots. Within it lies a seed, embryo, or the unrealized individual. Below, a spring with three-and-one-half spirals symbolizes latent kundalini energy. The doors are a birth canal or exit to the surface, where one can slowly advance. The eye is one's badge of cultural affiliation. The mother gives birth to us, while the elephant carries tradition. The *ankh* means we return to the soil at death.

— Walk solid with feet on the ground
— Healthy pride of heritage
— Harmony with parents
— Comfortable place to call home
— Enjoy being in nature (with plants, animals, etc)
— Attend to factual practicalities
— Content with life's daily essentials
— Access to resources
— Align with life's cycles and seasons

2ND CHAKRA

At center, the young ego sails a boat. The *makara* (monster) prowls below. Chests on the sea floor are a trap, a treasure, and trash (hidden baggage). The ego has a spear (its talent), and it must dive with it and explore to get the treasure. Islands on the side, like faces, suggest self-conscious awareness of others' stares and also sex roles and relations. Both, half-submerged, hold sexual allure. The world is full of life: We can plant, catch, grow, and/or create. In the sky, the sun, moon, star, and cloud are nature's touchstones. The big frame is the world, one's body, and also one's psyche.

— Curious with a drive to explore
— Solve puzzles and assess dangers well
— Harmony with friends
— Aware of and adjust to how others' perceive and react to you
— Physically fit with healthy lifestyle
— Tap your talents
— Participate in male/female sex roles
— Emotional maturity, few hang-ups, deal with baggage

3RD CHAKRA

"Truth" breaks the outer frame in the upper right corner. Truth is an all-seeing eye that offers divine pronouncements. The stalwart knight at center is our resilient ego. It faces toward Truth. By Truth's tablet of laws, the ego divides the world into four quadrants. The upper right hosts a holy angel (Truth's messenger). Three good people (the illuminated) sing in the upper left, while three bad people (the endarkened) bark in the lower right. The lower left contains a crowd of terrifying demons led by a devil to represent the untamed and terrifying unconscious. Flames motivate, ward, and guide us.

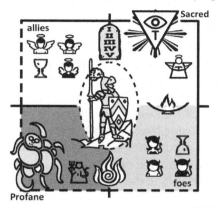

— Know your identity and values
— Energized to take action
— Life holds meaning and purpose
— Confidently move toward goals/ideals
— Stand firm for what matters to you
— Identify foes/allies without making them into idols, angels, or demons
— Part of an intentional community
— Stay informed without falling prey to slogans and wishful thinking

4TH CHAKRA

At center, the ego appears as two embracing hearts. Each complements the other. One is black, one is white, and each holds a small measure of the other (as a small circle) within itself. The tree's trunk and roots provide stability while branches reach into the open sky. The trunk is etched with old love notes. Fruit of love hangs from the tree. The world cycles through seasons, just as love supports and survives though life's changes. Tempting fruit on the tree in spring become a basket of edibles in summer, a harvested meal in fall, and emptiness in winter. The foundation is "LOVE."

— Give practical care to others
— Give loving kindness to all beings
— Willing to be vulnerable
— Keep others' vulnerability safe
— Enjoy a long-term romantic coupling
— Nurture (shepherd) children, students, mentees, or similar folk
— Emotionally honest to self and others
— Treat other people as unique human beings with talents and faults like you

5TH CHAKRA

The outer dotted frame and perimeter of words indicate freedom to explore using language. The bird soaring above the clouds symbolizes a capacity to see the world, including ourselves, from any angle. The meter acts as a reference point. In the thought bubble, we name where we are. The couple at center speak to each other, listening with ears perked. The wavy lines are blowing wind. Heat rises from the lower chakras via a flume, which is also a throat, to generate the wind. The windmill harnesses the wind for work, while the book represents education, knowledge, and learning.

— Communicate clearly
— Persuade/inspire with honest words
— Listen patiently to what others say
— Look at situations from several views
— Define what you see and hear and follow reason to find a solution
— Create using language (stories, poetry, arguments, laws, models, etc)
— Examine yourself objectively
— Let models and data guide decisions

6A CHAKRA

The psyche is a three-eyed monarch. The ego has built itself into an idol, cyborg, superhero, or such. The right hand sports money. The coin safely contains one's *anima* (or *animus* if female). The left hand sports a tesseract, symbolizing complexity. The third eye sits as a crown that grants wisdom, a will to create the future, and a deep working understanding of the world. The city, satellite in orbit, and globe stand for one's self and the world as a system. The owl lets us see and strike even in darkness. The throne of prosperity is our reward for integrity. The outer frame is a placeholder for the current era.

— Act with integrity
— Actively unmask illusions and deceptions (i.e. "follow the money")
— Test yourself to stay humble
— Stay tuned-in to your conscience
— Think systems, not just intentions: inputs, processes, and consequences
— Master your tools like a professional
— Seek win-win solutions
— Lead across conflicting groups

6B Chakra

The dotted frame means open boundaries. Within, psychedelic images from the unconscious run riot. The alien couple represent *anima* and *animus*, the hidden archetypical man or woman within us that aids growth. They stand within a flowering lotus, which symbolizes the flow of kundalini energy. The snake and moon are female archetypes. The cactus and rocket are male ones. The breathless stars are yet more psychical elements. The eye stands for lucid dreaming. The mirror means self-reflection. There is no sun. After all, this is the unconscious. Instead, a luminous crystal presides above it all.

— Expand your horizons with travel and workshops, for lifelong learning
— Engage in creative projects
— Attend to psychological patterns/ habits in yourself and others
— Explore altered states of consciousness and journal those experiences
— Integrate opposing forces, motives, and values within yourself
— Explore some healthy alter egos

7th Chakra

The frame is manifold, faint, and dotted. We float within the Divine, reeturning to our Source. The multiple frames are shifts in reality, and we and existence are vibrating. The curtain that normally separates the world and divine mystery is parted, at least for a time. There is no single ego, only conscious awareness indicated by the large eye at the top, which crowns the circles below it. Those circles are the chakras. The intertwining circular and radiating lines are freely flowing streams of kundalini energy. They also stand for physical and psychological energy fields. They are in constant motion.

— Acknowledge your spiritual need
— Seek a "kundalini awakening" or similar direct experience of the Divine
— Follow daily practices to stay "awake"
— Renounce worldly distractions, false identifications, and harmful habits
— Focus on your core life mission
— Be fully present with a quiet mind
— Open and align all the other chakras
— Act as a spiritual guide

Your Chakra Profile

Now that you've explored the chakras, use the table below to record your scores for each. High scores usually indicate a well-working chakra, or possibly an overactive chakra. Conversely, low scores usually indicate a blocked chakra. Chakras in between likely have room for improvement.

Use the table and scores to consider which chakras you want to target with mindful activities.

Center*		No.	Name & Element	Themes	Self-Rating
Spiritual	Adept	7	**Crown** *sahasrāra* Light	Unity & Awakening	_____ (page 66)
Spiritual	Basic	6B	**Third Eye** *ājñā* Ether	Psyche & Imagination	_____ (page 60)
Mental	Adept	6A	**Third Eye** *ājñā* Metal	Vision & Systems	_____ (page 54)
Mental	Basic	5	**Throat** *vishuddha* Air	Speech & Reason	_____ (page 48)
Emotional	Adept	4	**Heart** *anāhata* Wood	Balance & Empathy	_____ (page 42)
Emotional	Basic	3	**Solar Plexus** *manipūra* Fire	Action & Projection	_____ (page 36)
Physical	Adept	2	**Sacral** *svādhishthāna* Water	Danger & Renewal	_____ (page 30)
Physical	Basic	1	**Root** *mūlādhāra* Earth	Soil & Seed	_____ (page 24)

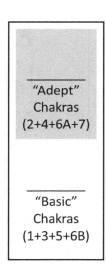

"Adept" Chakras (2+4+6A+7)

_____

"Basic" Chakras (1+3+5+6B)

* On the far left, the table organizes the chakras into four centers: physical, emotional, mental, and spiritual, each having two tiers, which I call here *basic* and *adept*. This is another way to organize the chakras.

Part 3

Yoga Plus

This section offers ways to work with chakras. You will find basic kundalini yoga exercises and suggestions to get the most from a kundalini awakening. There is a brief review of Jung's thoughts on *tantric* yoga and a chakra checklist for couples. A tour of the nervous system provides a scientific basis for the chakras. Also, there are other traditions similar to chakra work including Buddhist and Christian monastic practices. Finally, you will learn about entheogens (powerful shamanic medicines) to activate and align chakras.

Kundalini Basics

Chakra work is limited without physical activity. Yoga is a daily practice toward spiritual growth, to nurture a daily link to the Divine. To better understand the various ideas in this book and make progress on your spiritual journey, you probably want to get started with your own practice. Reading by itself is not enough and may easily lead to misunderstandings. Remember, words are the domain of the 5th chakra, and while that is a great space to be in, it is only part of the picture!

Getting Started

First, set aside a block of time, with no pressures, and find a quiet comfortable space with no intrusions. It generally takes 10 minutes for people to start to relax, to surrender the day's cares, so ideally spend 30 minutes to an hour. But do not look at a clock! Just set aside that time. And when that's not so easy, 10 minutes a day is better than nothing. A typical kundalini class is 90 minutes.

Second, wear loose clothing and gather items to aid your practice. A yoga cushion is helpful if you are unused to sitting on the floor. Outside, bare feet with a water feature is especially nice. You may have gentle music playing. The Internet offers streaming yoga music for free. Alternatively, some people prefer nature sounds or silence. Have drinking water close by.

Third, form your intention. The intention might be awakening, contentment, gratitude, health, happiness, insight, peace, or something similar. An intention is not a goal and you are welcome to phrase your intention as a question. Consider writing down questions you have. Whatever you do, once you actually start, put them away and let whatever comes up gently happen.

Finally, do some stretching and warm-up exercises. Rub down your muscles, your arms, legs, neck, and so forth, each time rubbing your hands together first to generate heat.

Basic Exercises

Kundalini exercises are called *kriya*. There are hundreds of them. Each kriya consists of several elements, including posture, breathing, hand and finger positions, spinal alignments, visualizations, and/or sacred sounds. When the elements are aligned, their impact exceeds their sum. The box on the facing page describes a few simple kriya you can try. Do each exercise for 2 to 10 minutes. Then rest for 30 seconds before repeating it or doing another exercise.

Whatever the exercise, attend to your posture. Start by sitting squarely on your butt with spine and head straight. Avoid sitting on your lower back, bowing your spine, or tilting your head. With today's constant focus on computer work, just maintaining posture is its own ongoing exercise!

All of the exercises have the same aim—to move energy. And the results? Quiet your monkey mind, diffuse the tension of everyday cares, focus on body awareness, move blood through your breathing and posture, prompt nerve pathways, and stimulate hormonal activity. Of course, a particular exercise may activate a specific chakra area or such.

Kundalini Yoga Exercises

Here are a few mindful activities, called *kriya,* to do during your kundalini yoga sessions.

1. **Tuning In**. There are many kundalini chants, or *mantras*. Kundalini begins with *Ong namo guru dev namo*. It roughly means, "tune to the Sacred within," or "I bow to the infinite Creator and givers of divine teachings." Chant it or an equivalent at least 3x when you start.
2. **Sufi Grinds**. Sit cross-legged, grab your kneecaps, and rotate your torso, keeping your head nearly still and putting pressure at the base of your spine. Reverse direction after 1 minute.
3. **Nostril Breathing**. Close your eyes. Use your index finger to close one nostril. With your mouth closed, breathe in slowly while counting to 10. Then hold and breathe out slowly counting to 10. Repeat three times. Then switch to the other nostril and repeat.
4. **Heaven and Earth**: Is your intent to get grounded in the present moment and still your monkey mind? Or is your intent to gain insight into a problem? For grounding, breathe slowly and deeply, counting to three with each step; breathe in, hold it, and exhale, and all along, keep focusing your attention on your belly, feeling the weight of your body and earth. For insight, as you breathe, keep focusing your attention on your head and the heavens above instead.
5. **Cat Cow**. Get on your hands and knees. Place your hands under your shoulders and your knees under your hips. Raise your head up while pushing your belly down. Inhale deeply while doing so. Then bring your head down with your chin toward your chest and arch your back up. Exhale as you do this. Repeat slowly, then speed up, for 2—3 minutes. When done, relax on your heels.
6. **Eternal Cycle**. Another *mantra* is *Sa Ta Na Ma*. Roughly, it means "birth, life, death, rebirth." While chanting each syllable, lightly flex each of 4 fingers to your thumb, from index to pinky. Chant for at least 2 minutes. Once you finish, repeat but in a softer voice and then again silently to yourself. These 3 phases represent action, words, and spirit.
7. **1-Minute Breath**. Very slowly you breathe, nose only, counting to 20. Then hold for 20 seconds and release very slowly for 20 seconds, nose only. If you cannot get to 20, try 10 seconds each. Repeat 10x. Your mind will inevitably slow and get quiet as it syncs to your breathing.
8. **Breath of Fire**. For this exercise, you breathe in and out very rapidly through your nose only. Breathe deeply into your lower lungs, one breath per second. One, two, three... up to 30, or 60 if you can. Each second, grow your belly and then let it bounce back as you exhale.
9. **Bearing Down**. Close your eyes, pressing your lids firmly against your eyeballs, and curl your tongue to touch the roof of your mouth. Next, fill your lungs, pinch your nose, and bear down as if popping your ears when rising or descending in an airplane. Bear down as long as you can.
10. **Mandala Focus**. A *mandala* is a symbolic spiritual image. There are many throughout all cultures, both Eastern and Western. Their complex patterns can evoke unconscious reactions. Place a mandala image before you, then close your eyes 3/4 of the way (or 90% if you can) and gaze at the mandala. Contemplate its shapes, patterns, colors. Whatever interruptions occur, keep returning your gaze to the mandala image. Do this for 5—15 minutes.

Flowing Upward

Kundalini exercises generally proceed in three phases: lower body, mid-body, and head. You go from your toes to your crown, following the chakras.

Start with your lower body, moving your legs, freeing up your hip muscles, and so forth. Leg lifts with some rotation are a simple start, then you might work your abdominal muscles. You likely know many such exercises from the gym, but pay extra attention to your breathing and add a *mantra*. For example, when doing squats add *Sat* (pronounced "saht") when descending and *Nam* (pronounced "nahm") when ascending, and breathe in and out through your nose exactly in time to your ups and downs. These extras help quiet your mind and move energy in a uniform, efficient way. Afterward, as a reward for this hard work, sit very still in lotus position for a few minutes to relax.

Next, focus on the mid-body. For example, rotate your arms like a windmill while doing the Breath of Fire (#8 on the previous page). Or you may add an intention, such as using your arm motions to pull out and expel negative energy, such as from a scuffle from earlier in the day. Or, rub your hands together and lay them over your heart, pressing firmly (right hand over left) while chanting and holding a loving image in your mind's eye. You will be warm by now, and this will feel very nice. This is an example of installing a *vinyasa*. That word means "to place in a special way." At each chakra point, you can install a way you would like it to be, using a mantra, visualization, and such. There is much you can do beyond the scope of this introduction. Yoga teachers know many exercises and installation options.

Finally, move up to your head. This may start with head rotation and throat work—singing or fierce breathing. But this phase ends quietly, a reward after a long workout. Lie still and allow yourself to descend into a deep, relaxing place. Optionally, use this time to progressively focus on your body. Start with your feet, feeling your toes and ankles, then slowly move upward, listening closely to your body and allowing each part to awaken as you tighten and then relax it. Stay patient. You may feel tingling, jitters, or warmth in an area. Allow any sensations to manifest completely and release them before continuing up your body. You may stop a few or many times. What is important is that you are becoming aware of your body's energy system and allowing it to realign and flow freely.

Commitment to Awakening

Kundalini yoga is a deceptively simple path. Sessions will be varied, light, and fun; and then, after a few months of practice, you will likely experience a genuine shift in your state of consciousness. This may occur during a yoga session or at some other time. When this occurs, a sudden activation of energy, a shocking insight, or torrent of emotion can result in joy, peace, confusion, or distress. Thus, it is important to have a teacher when venturing beyond the basics.

Meaningful results take commitment and discipline. Even if you've come to know altered states of consciousness using entheogens (pages 94-98), daily practices are necessary to carry over benefits into everyday life long-term. Minimally, strive for 40 consecutive days of yoga or a similar meditative practice. Missing a day is okay but not ideal; if you do, add a week to your program. And on a given day, if you cannot do an hour or 30 minutes, do 5 minutes just to keep the habit familiar.

Kundalini Awakening

Kundalini yoga helps release the latent energy within each of us. This release often happens gradually in various ways. Exercise and awareness help us learn to be more mindful and literally get in touch with and move our own energy. Over time, we can become more present physically, emotionally, mentally, and spiritually. Occasionally, however, a person's latent energy may release all at once in a huge blast. This sudden, massive release is called a kundalini *awakening*.

What happens during a kundalini awakening? How do you know you are having the experience? And what do you do when it happens?

People use words like "amazing," "disorienting," "powerful," and "surprising" to describe the awakening. It manifests physically. You feel energy all over your body, typically starting from the groin and emanating upwards through the crown. A pillar of energy may zoom up and down the spine. You may feel you are projecting energy into the air or down into the ground. Other common indicators include sweating, warmth, tingling, twitching, and vibrating all over. You may easily feel like an antenna conducting so much energy that you can barely contain it. At the same time, it manifests mentally. You likely experience a flood of insights, renewed passion for living, and a feeling of unity within yourself and with others, Nature, and the Divine. Your thinking and purpose are clearer and more consistent, reduced to their essential essence. You focus on *now*. The energy release and insights easily last for several days. You need little sleep. Whatever the specifics, you may feel you are on drugs, suffering a strange crisis, or channeling a spiritual power. An awakening might even be mistakenly diagnosed as a psychotic episode, though it is not violent or such.

The more prepared you are for a kundalini awakening, the more rewarding it will be. Yoga is a great way to prepare. A full awakening involves all the chakras. Energy wells up from the 1st chakra and washes through all the others to the crown. Any and all blockages are temporarily blown through. Thus, it is much more than a meditative reverie. If you have done yoga and chakra work, the experience will be pleasurable and enlightening. Your body and mind will be prepared to handle the energy release. Having a book, friend, teacher, or other guide who has already awakened also helps. Have a confidante who can give your feedback about appropriate behavior. For example, in the middle of it all, you might feel moved to make a major announcement or change in your life that will have unwanted consequences later. Minimally, a book like this at least helps you know what is occurring so you can ride through it with curiosity and some peace of mind.

Scientifically speaking, what happens during an awakening? No one is precisely sure. However, as described under "The Nervous System" (pages 84-91), kundalini practices closely mirror medical techniques to activate the Vagal Nerve System (VNS). This system runs from the brain down through all the body's major organs. These organs mirror the chakras. Activating the VNS promotes relaxation in all of those organs. Moreover, it dampens the fight-or-flight response and other aggressive, fearful, and neurotic behaviors generated by our primitive animal brain—the limbic system. You can learn more about these organs and brain regions later in this chapter.

You may experience partial kundalini awakenings before or after a full awakening. A partial experience may involve one side of the body—the top or bottom half only—or, more often, a specific chakra. For example, the area around your heart may suddenly "catch fire," blazing with an inner warmth. Thereafter, it feels acutely exposed. This feeling of raw exposure may be the source of terms like *open* versus *closed* chakra. In the same area, you might also register stabs of pain, such as a crown of thorns or the stab of a sword. You will likely also find yourself more sensitive to your own and others' emotions, as suggested by the heart chakra. For the person experiencing this, the feeling is quite plainly not heartburn or some other medical problem. Rather, the nerve bundles in that area are likely alight with activity as they link to the conscious mind. These links may be reactivating for the very first time in the person's adult life. Long after a full kundalini awakening, people can continue to experience similar partial awakenings for each of the chakras. It is also possible that a person will only ever experience a series of partial awakenings.

A kundalini awakening is not the endpoint of kundalini yoga. It is not even necessary for a healthy, happy, and holy life. It is, however, a life-changing gateway. The contrast between before and after is huge. Before the awakening, a person may feel as if he or she has lived in a hypnotic sleep-like trance of ordinary life. With the awakening, they gain a heightened state of calm alertness and flowing energy that feels very clear. In the months and years after awakening, the memories of it will last, although life's distractions and stressors will challenge them to stay awake. This is where the real work starts. Fortunately, awakened persons have preceded us and developed practices such as kundalini yoga to help us make the most of our new situation.

How can we best encourage and sustain an awakening? Foremost, practice kundalini yoga. It is designed specifically for this task! Similar practices, such as *tantric* yoga, can also help. Dedicate yourself to a daily practice, even if you meditate or such only ten minutes a day. You can even meditate on insights gained during an awakening, focusing on both the bodily sensations and the mental images or sounds you experienced. Those who "stay awake" say they feel a tingling sensation most of the time in the back of their head, or even all over their body, when they just focus for a moment. For sure, set aside time that's free of work, technology, consumerism, and media. Also consider shamanic journeys and/or nature retreats. Avoid negative people and situations, party drugs and alcohol, and prolonged high stress. Basically, quietly embrace whatever helps you feel awake, shining, and vibrant while gently staying away from anything that leaves you feeling like a dull, tired zombie.

Whether you choose to stay awake or to fall asleep again, there are consequences. In the film *The Matrix*, the main character Neo is presented with a blue pill and a red pill. He is informed, if "you take the blue pill, the story ends. You wake up in your bed and believe whatever you want to believe." However, if "you take the red pill, you stay in Wonderland, and I show you how deep the rabbit hole goes." In the film, the red pill refers to a human being who is aware of the true nature of his enslavement within the illusion of the Matrix and the chance for liberation from that illusion. Returning to the illusion is actually the easier choice. Liberation is harder. After taking the red pill, Neo had to face tremendous challenges and responsibilities. Similarly, as yoga teachers say, embracing your kundalini awakening will ask a lot more of you as you go forward.

Tantric Yoga

In addition to kundalini yoga, Dr. Jung delved into *tantra* yoga starting with a 1930 lecture, which appears in Appendix I of Shamdasani's *The Psychology of Kundalini Yoga*.

Tantra focuses on harmonizing and exchanging female and male divine energies, both within a person and as a couple. Female energy, called *yoni*, means the "source of all life" or "sacred space." In contrast, male energy, or *linga,* means a "shaft of light" or a "mark," "emblem," or "sign." These two energies are often symbolized by the goddess Shakti and the god Shiva in Hinduism, or as *yin* and *yang* in Taoism. In each of us, one energy is more conscious and dominant, but both are present and needed, and yoga acknowledges and works with them, internally and maybe with another person.

The ultimate goal of tant*ra* is the productive union of these two sexual energies, of Shakti and Shiva. The word *tantra* in Sanskrit means "expansion" or "weaving," which reminds us that it is not necessarily about having sex. The genitals involve just one or two chakras. Tantra aims to utilize all the chakras to help awaken and share energy and, with practice, both people enjoy a full-bodied ecstatic experience that is created through the alignment of all the chakras between them.

There is both art and science to tant*ra*. In yoga, artists often depict the dance of energies as entwining energy lines that course up the body. The lines start at the spine's base, weave up through each chakra, and merge at the head where they explode in pure radiant energy. From a scientific view, these two energies are like the two modes of the autonomic nervous system (ANS): the excited fight-or-flight mode versus the relaxed eat-or-sleep mode. These two modes suffuse all bodily organs, stimulating different responses from each gland or organ. Being one-sided, such as always in a fight mode, is unhealthy. Instead, balance is key for physical, emotional, and mental health. In particular, sex needs both modes for a full experience. You must be both excited and relaxed.

Jung analyzed tant*ra* through the lenses of alchemy and archetypes. Throughout his career, he spoke about common archetypes such as the Wise Mother, Trickster, Warrior Hero, and so forth. Many archetypes have a male or female energy, and chief among these is the *anima* (a man's inner unconscious feminine force) and the *animus* (a woman's inner unconscious masculine force). Even within us, we carry our opposite. A woman carries both her own conscious energy and an unconscious male potential, and vice versa for a man. We can bring these complementary energies together through spiritual practices and through our intimate relationships. And from the tension of opposites, creative energy is born, and it is through the union of opposites that transcendence and awakening occur*.

Tantra practices are beyond this book's scope. Briefly, like kundalini, start by making a pleasing space. Add natural elements like fire and water. Next, focus on breathwork. Synchronize and share your breath. To remain more "present," limit speaking and eye contact, merely stealing glimpses. Take it slow and "dance" together as you build up your energies. Use touch to channel energy. Abstain from instant gratification as you awaken sexual energy from the base of the spine and bring it up into your bodies. You will warm up, tingle, and maybe enter an altered state. The benefit is more than heightened sex. It merges two persons—two psyches—to promote creativity, growth, healing, and love.

* *Letters Vol. 1* by C. G. Jung, et al. Princeton University Press, 1973, page 269.

Chakras for Couples

The graphic at right represents a couple and their chakras. For intimate relationships, each chakra offers unique challenges and rewards. Moreover, each person's chakras are more or less open and active in positive or negative ways. Thus, we connect in many ways. You can use the graphic as a lens to analyze a current or past relationship. Where are the fits and mis-fits? You can use it as a guide to locate how you—or you two—may grow into a more satisfying relationship. You can also describe what kind of relationship might suit you better in the future.

The graphic is organized with persons on the left and right and the gifts of each chakra in the middle. It is general. For details, reread the chakra descriptions in Part 2. Notice the little boxes. Rate each chakra on a scale of 1 to 5, where 5 is most healthy. (Or, more simply, enter "✓" for healthy chakras and "x" for unhealthy chakras.) When in doubt about a rating, heed your initial gut response.

Each chakra can play out in a relationship in one of four ways, as summarized in the matrix below. For each chakra, refer to the matrix to determine the kind of dynamic that is going on.

	Partner: Healthy Chakra	Partner: Unhealthy Chakra
You: Healthy Chakra	**Light**: For both of you, joyful, easy, fruitful, mature, energizing, with mutual attraction that aids your lives' work.	**Mixed: You** are frustrated, tired, and fill needs elsewhere. **Partner** is oblivious and projects wishes/fears onto you.
You: Unhealthy Chakra	**Mixed: Partner** is frustrated, tired, and fills needs elsewhere. **You** are oblivious and project wishes/fears onto partner.	**Dark**: For both of you, a shared blindspot, emptiness, fanaticism, fear, and/or silent on issues with no resolution.

What do the dynamics mean? A chakra may act as a joyful and creative point when it is open and healthy for both people. For example, a healthy 5th chakra for both is a point of light with great communication. Oppositely, a chakra may be a shared blindspot; it is a dark, dormant link that never seems to bear fruit. For example, if both people are closed at the 2nd chakra, they will likely suffer a boring sex life and stale socializing. For the two mixed spots, there is a clash. For example, one person may have a healthy 3rd chakra with mature self-confidence to take action while the other keeps trying to play out a passive victim role or, oppositely, be fanatical and aggressive. Whatever the imbalance, the person with the healthy chakra is frustrated while the other is unconsciously framing his or her partner as an angel or devil.

This is a quick peek into the roles chakras can play in relationships. The main point: It takes all chakras, not just the heart chakra, to enjoy a great relationship. Moreover, while it is possible for amazingly mature people to find a perfect fit, it is more likely we couple with a mishmash of chakras, perhaps with an eye at times on those who offer a different mishmash. Many challenges fester in the 2nd chakra. If you want to explore further, there are several solid books that focus on this topic.

Chakra Checklist for Couples

Rate on a 1 to 5 scale, with 5 as healthiest.

Partner A

Partner B

#7. Crown
Unity & Awakening: Open to spiritual growth, has an ongoing relationship to the Divine, resists glamor, affirms life.

#6B. Third Eye
Psyche & Imagination: Creative, explores and experiments, manages stress, sense of humor, magical.

#6A. Third Eye
Vision & Systems: Acts with integrity, wise parent and/or leader, clear-eyed, has deep principles, successful career.

#5. Throat
Speech & Reason: Easily communicates thoughts and feelings, listens well, self improves, educated, a life-long learner.

#4. Heart
Balance & Empathy: Cares for others, gives appropriate trust and respect, kind, affectionate, can be vulnerable.

#3. Solar Plexus
Action & Projection: Self-confident, knows and stands up for own values and beliefs, active but not overly aggressive.

#2. Sacral
Danger & Renewal: Healthy sexuality, free from hang-ups, has close friends, on good terms with family, physically fit.

#1. Root
Soil & Seed: Feet on the ground, sense of heritage, steady, offers security, deals well with hardship, able to settle down.

The Nervous System

Science helps explain how kundalini yoga works. The nervous system is an incredible set of organs and networks that acts as a substrate for the mind and psyche. And it is more than the brain. It runs throughout the body and is both electrical and chemical, generating a myriad of signals, patterns, and fields within and around us. Here are some of the key players.

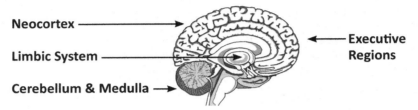

In Your Brain

Your brain consists of several evolutionary layers, organized into regions that help you with specific tasks. These regions all work together in a network. Hormones also play a big role.

Executive Regions: These key brain regions sit behind the forehead. If the brain were a company, these would be its two CEOs. Yes, two chiefs! The left executive is goal-focused. It gets active when we decide, explain, and filter out distractions. In contrast, the right executive is open-ended. It gets active when we brainstorm, seek stimulus, and reflect on data. Ideally, these two executives work well with each other. Using meditation or yoga, people can coordinate or quiet them.

Neocortex: The "new brain" is unique to humans in its thickness and complexity. It is our seat of awareness and home to all we learn by education. It supports many skills including language, abstract perception, self-control, empathy, reasoning, tool use, foresight, and artistic and mathematical skills. Everyone develops somewhat differently here based on upbringing and daily habits.

Unconscious Conflicts

Where is the unconscious? It is all over the nervous system. Here are key ways it pops up.

- **Automatic behaviors**, which often lie outside awareness, may leave us feeling stuck in a loop or induce conflict with other people. Examples include body language and biases in word choice.
- **Inter-brain conflicts**, such as impulses from the more primitive limbic system pushing one thing while advice from the more recent, conscious, and educated neocortex pushes something else.
- **Under-utilized brain networks or suppressed memories** that lie outside our set of habits or self-definition may pop up randomly—when stressed, during therapy, or if relaxed or distracted.
- **Right-hemisphere activity**, which is mostly nonverbal, feels less accessible to us. We may notice its activity but we find its workings hard to express and easy to filter out of our awareness.
- **Energy patterns** are activated and/or stored throughout the nervous system in the body. These include muscle memory, glandular patterns, and gut hormones that influence our thinking.

Task and Default Networks: These are key brain networks. The task network (TN) gets active when we focus outward on activities such as using a device. In contrast, the default network (DN) gets active as a stream of conscious thoughts when we are not doing a task. Besides fantasy, the DN includes negative self-talk, us-versus-them thinking, and similar thought patterns. Keeping busy with a task quiets it. Meditation and yoga quiet it too while also giving us a neutral, observer viewpoint.

Limbic System: All mammals have this system. Its activity is mostly out of our awareness. It is a switching station for memory and home for instinct, family bonds, sexual attractions, addictions, phobias, and strong emotions such as fear, disgust, and hate. For example, when we feel threatened, it prompts us to fight or flee. Kundalini exercises stimulate the VNS (see box below) to dampen these reactions. This region also impacts motivation and learning. Whatever is scripted here, often in early childhood, will imprint strongly for life. Mental illnesses also have roots here.

Neurotransmitters: These are brain hormones such as dopamine and serotonin. They release through the brain very quickly and impact many aspects of behavior such as alertness, attention, focus, physical activity, and mood. Cells in various brain regions have receptors that these chemicals attach to. Studies show that everyday activities such as touching, exercise, and meditation can change the levels of these chemicals, perhaps within a few minutes.

Pineal and Pituitary Glands: These two hormone-producing organs sit snugly inside the brain. The pituitary sends signals and receives feedback from other glands. For example, it signals the gonads to produce sex hormones. It also impacts learning and social behavior. Above it, the pineal gland regulates sleep, dreams, wakefulness, and some altered states of consciousness. It also impacts learning. These glands are often linked to the 6th and 7th chakras.

Cerebellum and Medulla: These primitive bulbous masses support balance, breathing, hunger and thirst, temperature regulation, automatic behaviors like sneezing, and basic survival drives like reproduction and territory marking. These regions work automatically in the background but we can briefly override aspects of them, such as by changing our breathing in meditation or yoga.

Relaxing to Awaken
Modern treatments and ancient practices stimulate the Vagus Nerve System (VNS) to help us relax.

- Fight-or-flight stress and the anxiety of modern living suppress the VNS and inflict rapid shallow breathing, high heart rate, and impaired digestion.
- Studies show that the VNS elevates mood and shifts brain activity. (Specifically, it increases serotonin, norepinephrine, GABA and glutamate. The latter two you can buy at a market!)
- Vagus nerve stimulation therapy is medically approved to treat depression and epilepsy. Depression is often a symptom of other issues, and alleviating it can open a door to address those issues.
- You can relax with vagal maneuvers—such as holding your breath while bearing down (Valsalva maneuver), putting pressure on your eyelids, and massaging the carotid sinus area.
- Traditional spiritual practices such as deep breathing, yoga, and meditation also stimulate the VNS. Multiple religious traditions describe transcendent experiences when doing these.

Brain Regions, Meditation, and Yoga

Your brain consists of many small modules that link together. Each module is a neural circuit that *helps* you do a task. Some tasks are concrete, such as recognizing faces, hearing voice tone, and moving a hand. Other tasks are abstract, such as evaluating ethics, adjusting to others' feedback, and mentally rehearsing a future action. Naturally, to meet our needs, the modules work in concert. As an analogy, if a module is a musical instrument, then the brain is a symphony orchestra that affords complex performances. There are easily five dozen modules just in the neocortex, which is the brain's outermost, thick layer and seat of consciousness.

The big figure at right is a bird's eye view of the neocortex*. It highlights key modules (the map's labels are illustrative, not definitive). We each prefer some modules over others. We differ by the tasks we enjoy and how well we do them. For each of us, the modules activate with a different degree of stimulus, competence, motivation, and energy level. You might take a moment to explore the big figure and circle ten tasks that likely describe you well.

Our brain's two executives sit at the top of the map (labeled Fp1 and Fp2). The call-out boxes describe their main contributions. "Focused Judging" on the left helps us with many goal-oriented tasks such as making decisions. In contrast, "Curious Exploring" on the right helps us with many data-seeking and reflective tasks. The two usually work closely to get us through our day as they manage the whole rest of the brain. However, they also heavily filter and limit how we perceive and decide. Even if some other part of our brain registers critical data, such as a nearby danger, our executive regions may screen it out such that it fails to enter our awareness. Over the long-term, when our executives get rigid, they limit our consciousness and we get stuck in our ways.

Fortunately, mindfulness practices like meditation can turn down—or even disconnect—these executives for a time. When that happens, we may calm down—"whatever will be, will be." We may easily notice "what we already knew" when other brain regions finally get their signals through. If these executives have been out of balance, meditation may rebalance them and perhaps even give us an objective view of their workings. We can step back and observe our stream of thoughts, perceptions, and feelings without assigning meaning to them or judging ourselves.

What about kundalini yoga? Overall, it stimulates the whole brain! Firstly, performing whole-body exercises taps the brain's central regions (C3 and C4). Yoga tasks us to move the body, follow steps, and stay graceful while paying attention to our bodily sensations. Many kundalini kriyas also involve visualizing. For exmple, we might focus on a chakra or mandala in our mind's eye. These evoke visual brain regions (O1 and O2). Then there are *mantras* and music. Whether we chant aloud or repeat words quietly to ourselves, words and sounds stimulate the brain's auditory regions (T3 and T4). Kundalini also includes *mudras*, which are hand positions. Mudras are key. Brain regions that manage our hand motions (F3 and F4) are also heavily involved in mental planning, logical reasoning, and the use of concepts. Finally, regions like F8 may get active when the spiritual side of yoga stimulates brain regions linked to personal values and beliefs. In sum, all these facets of yoga easily engage half the brain, and kriyas can stimulate all the regions simultaneously for specific results. Research supports these shifts, mostly for experienced practitioners but also for novices.

Focused Judging (Fp1)
This help us...
Stay focused. Make decisions and select among options. Be results-oriented and sharp. Screen out distractions and criticism. Evaluate situations according to a principle. Notice and correct errors. Clarify needs, goals, and ideas. Get organized. Show confidence. With overuse, may be rigid and closed to input.

Curious Exploring (Fp2)
This help us...
Stay open to new data and experiences. Seek stimulating ideas and activities. Engage in a creative process. Mix and match. Navigate a situation and know when all ideas are in. Reflect on new data, delving into criticism for self-awareness. Show natural, honest expressions. With overuse, may get off-task.

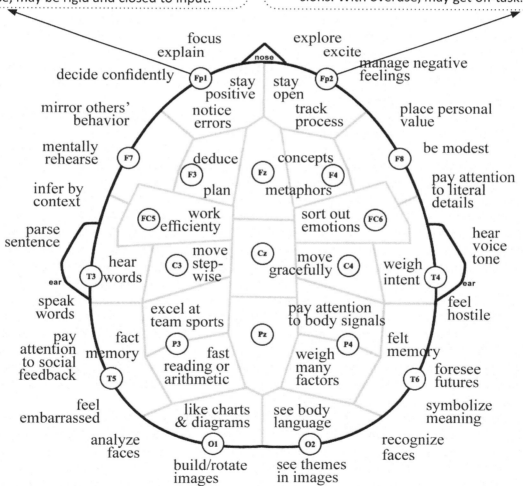

Figure 2: The brain aids us in many ways with all of our daily activities

* Neuroscience of Personality: Brain-Savvy Insights for All Types of People by Dario Nardi. Radiance House, 2011.

Brainwaves and Altered States

Throughout the day, we spend time in various brain states. To use a metaphor, each brain state is like a radio station, and each radio station has its own style from relaxing to exciting. Each brain state is made up of brainwaves, which have scientific Greek names like *delta* or *gamma*. Typically, all brainwaves are present during a task, but one or two predominate. Naturally, each brain state influences our consciousness. Five general states are described below, while the facing page compares two specific states—a typical daily routine versus an especially potent meditation. Of course, there are many meditative practices, each with its own benefits. As you read, consider how you tend to use your brain.

Insight Gamma: We show this state when we are very highly engaged in a task, working intensely, learning, and possibly excited. People also show this state when they notice someone they find attractive or when they experience an "aha!" insight. A particular task might only evoke a few brain regions to "go gamma". People who throw themselves completely into their creative tasks often show this state. Prolonged time here is balanced by exercise and deep sleep. Most people only spend a fraction of their day in this state.

Busy Beta: People show this state when their brains are alert, busy, and striving to solve a problem that requires some figuring out. Often, there is the promise of a reward. The reward might be an external offer or from an inner drive. As a problem gets challenging, we can easily move from busy to striving to stressed. All the while, we are focused, likely moving around, using our senses, and making progress on practical tasks. Naturally, we need genuine rest to balance this state, which easily predominates throughout a challenging working day.

Gut-Feel Alpha: This is a body-connected state. We often go here when we close our eyes and do an internal task such as listening to music, focusing on body sensations, attending to our gut instinct, recalling a past experience, or entertaining our imagination. This is fun when the music, memory or such is pleasing. However, we can feel bad if we focus on something negative. This state can act as a *gateway* to unconscious material, and it benefits us when we do yoga, work with chakras, or aim to change our habits. Some people get into this state more easily than others.

Routine Theta: We show this state when we are resting lightly or doing routine activities that we already know how to do. It has a slightly mindless or detached feeling to it. Its home to all our habitual thinking patterns. It can be practical. For example, we usually don't think about the details of driving a car. However, breaking routine can be challenging. People sometimes "retreat" to this state to avoid a negative feeling. We may spend a lot of time here when our day is boring or our mind is dulled by a mind-altering prescription drug.

Relaxed Delta: This state predominates during deep sleep. We also show a bit of it in the background throughout our day. For example, many daily tasks only require high participation of a few brain regions, so even when we are highly engaged, some brain areas are silent. People also go here when they enjoy "creative flow," doing something they really enjoy and are skilled at. This follows the saying, "You are so good, you can do it in your sleep!" It is like easy listening music with the volume turned up to maximum.

* *Your Brain in Altered States* [PDF] by Dario Nardi. http://www.Facebook.com/NeuroTypes

Real-Time Brain Changes

When people do yoga, meditate—or, as we will soon see, work with *entheogens* or otherwise enter an altered state—their brain changes. We can see these changes live on a neuro-imaging device as they do the exercises*.

Firstly, brainwaves change. Like radio channels, we can tune to specific brain frequencies like alpha waves, gamma waves, and so forth. Each has a meaning as described earlier. The two charts below compare typical baseline brain activity versus a trained body-mind brain activity. (The measurements are in mVolts vs. Hertz.)

Over time, body-mind practices can rewrite us. In our daily routine, we tend to focus our attention and respond in habitual ways, moment-to-moment, day in and out. We can feel stuck or caught in a loop. The loop might be helpful, or not. Happily, exercises can help us forge new, more-satisfying networks, perhaps in surprising ways such as a whole-brain pattern for creativity.

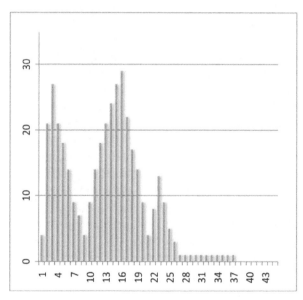

"Task Stress" Brain Activity

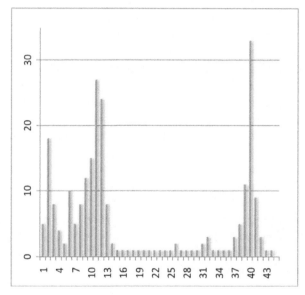

Body-Mind Brain Activity

Here, a person is going about daily tasks with eyes open. The left-most peak in the chart shows high delta and theta waves: either resting or engaging in routine tasks on autopilot in a detached way. The big middle peak is beta waves: the person is busy and may be challenged to meet goals or is stressed.

Here, an expert is sitting or lying down with eyes closed in a state of deep meditation. The left-most little spike indicates rest. The next left spike is alpha waves for mental activity with a body connection, when thoughts and feelings align. The right-most spike is high frequency gamma waves to gain insights and engage in learning.

Throughout Your Body

The nervous system runs throughout the whole body, linking it to every patch and crevice of your body inside and out, including hormone-producing glands and other organs. Consider that 80% of these nerves run from the body into the brain; only 20% run the other way. Hormones also strongly impact mental and emotional life in addition to physical traits.

Autonomic Nervous System (ANS): These nerves link the brain and other organs. They suffuse the face, tongue, throat, heart, lungs, solar plexus, stomach, colon, gonads, and more. The *sympathetic* side of the ANS promotes an excited fight-or-flight mode, while the *parasympathetic* side, including the Vagus Nerve System, puts us in a relaxed eat-or-sleep mode. With effort, we can consciously regulate the ANS, such as taking 10 minutes of deep, slow breaths in order to calm ourselves. A "kundalini awakening" can make us acutely hyper-aware of the activity of the ANS. On the opposite page, the dotted "conveyer belt" from head to groin represents the flow of data in the ANS.

Heart: This is more than a pump. It sustains an electromagnetic field around us and is a gauge of our breathing. Anyone can speed up or slow down their breathing, and within 10 minutes of concentrated effort, the brain will follow the heart's change of pace. Two people can bring their heart beats into synch. No surprise, it is the 4th chakra! Page 11, under "Your Core Self," more fully describes the physical field produced by your heart that radiates outward by several feet.

Endocrine Glands: The five hormone-producing glands that sit in the torso include the gonads, pancreas, adrenals, thymus, and thyroid. They impact physical traits, mood, and many other characteristics. For example, the thyroid promotes fast mental activity along with a faster metabolism in general. The glands work both briefly and over long periods. They produce hormones based on signals from the pituitary, other brain regions, and the ANS. These glands are often linked to the 1st through 5th chakras. The figure on the opposite page describes key features of the seven endocrine glands. You can learn more about the endocrine glands from Dr. Laura Power at www.biotype.net/types.

Gut: Your gut is your second brain. It is a major source of brain hormones such as such as serotonin that impact mood, thinking, and health. What you eat, and how you eat, greatly impact your health and happiness. For example, eating relaxes us while stress impairs digestion.

Motor / Sensory Nerves: These link our skin, muscles, and senses to our brain and glands. We may only notice extreme stimuli or be hypersensitive. We can hone our awareness and skill.

Emotions, Trauma, and the Body: Does the body record our emotional experiences? Can we access and modify that record? Can we heal for our peace of mind? In survival situations, we can go from calm to fight-or-flight to a complete shutdown very quickly. Because mind and body closely link, such intense moments involve the whole self. The brain easily records the event in its memory networks, and later when the memory is triggered, related networks through the body can also reactivate. The result can be Post Traumatic Stress Disorder, among other manifestations. Researchers like Lauri Nummenmass have developed *Bodily Maps of Emotions* (Proceedings of the National Academy of Sciences, 2014). Similarly, clinicians like Dr. Bessel van der Kolk have developed treatment techniques as explained in *The Body Keeps the Score: Brain, Mind, and Body in the Healing of Trauma*.

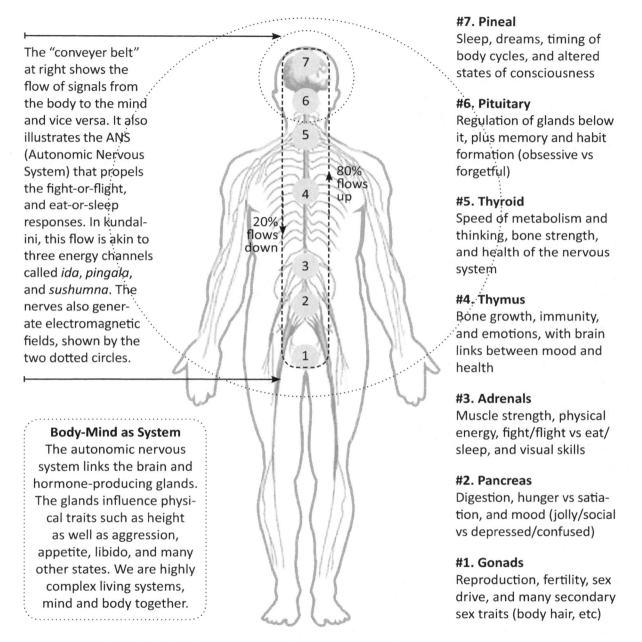

#7. Pineal
Sleep, dreams, timing of body cycles, and altered states of consciousness

#6. Pituitary
Regulation of glands below it, plus memory and habit formation (obsessive vs forgetful)

#5. Thyroid
Speed of metabolism and thinking, bone strength, and health of the nervous system

#4. Thymus
Bone growth, immunity, and emotions, with brain links between mood and health

#3. Adrenals
Muscle strength, physical energy, fight/flight vs eat/sleep, and visual skills

#2. Pancreas
Digestion, hunger vs satiation, and mood (jolly/social vs depressed/confused)

#1. Gonads
Reproduction, fertility, sex drive, and many secondary sex traits (body hair, etc)

The "conveyer belt" at right shows the flow of signals from the body to the mind and vice versa. It also illustrates the ANS (Autonomic Nervous System) that propels the fight-or-flight, and eat-or-sleep responses. In kundalini, this flow is akin to three energy channels called *ida*, *pingala*, and *sushumna*. The nerves also generate electromagnetic fields, shown by the two dotted circles.

7

6

5

80% flows up

4

20% flows down

3

2

1

Body-Mind as System
The autonomic nervous system links the brain and hormone-producing glands. The glands influence physical traits such as height as well as aggression, appetite, libido, and many other states. We are highly complex living systems, mind and body together.

Figure 3: Endocrine glands and the nerve system link throughout the body

Other Traditions

Besides kundalini yoga, there are other ways—ancient and modern—to awaken and transform. Other schools of yoga refer to the chakras. There is also breathwork, desensitization, meditation, monasticism, and shamanism, all of which tap the chakras in some way and have a scientific element to their practices. Here is a brief summary of four methods.

Christian Monasticism

In Christianity, the Eastern Orthodox Church officially supports *Hesychasm*, a mystical practice dating back to at least the 13th century. This practice emphasizes contemplative prayer and exercise to achieve "an experiential knowledge of God."

Monks embark on a three-step process: purification, illumination, and finally divine union. The process cultivates mindfulness, or "watchful attention," and focuses on chanting the Jesus Prayer to "obliterate" distracting thoughts. The goal is to align one's actions and words, mind and heart with divine will. Practice involves postures and breathing techniques to submerge the mind into the heart. Hesychast monks describe the ultimate ecstatic union using the same language that yoga and Dr. Jung have used to describe the crown chakra. The monk enters the "Uncreated Light" described by Saint Gregory Palamas and is filled with the Holy Spirit. As part of training, the monk is tasked to stay humble and avoid "spiritual delusion" that might be egotistical.

Dr. Jung was apparently unaware of Hesychasm. However, he did say, "the West will produce its own Yoga and it will be on the basis laid down by Christianity." Modern writers are now linking Jungian psychology with this ancient practice, spreading the benefits of "praying with the body."

The Fourth Way*

A contemporary of Dr. Jung, Armenian philosopher George Ivanovich Gurdjieff developed a system to awaken, and to stay awake. Often called "the Work" or "the System," he described an alternative to the hypnotic state of "waking sleep" that most people seemed to live in.

During years of travel, Gurdjieff studied techniques of yogis, monks, and fakirs. His "Fourth Way" synthesizes these to address "the question of humanity's place in the Universe and the possibilities of inner development." He taught that a "higher level of consciousness, virtue, and unity of will are all possible." This Fourth Way "teaches how to increase and focus attention and energy in various ways" and this "is the beginning of a possible further process of change, whose aim is to transform Man into 'what he ought to be.'" The practices focus on "conscious labor," which means being fully present in the moment, and on "intentional suffering," which involves turning away urges that lead into vices, including learning to "endure the displeasing manifestations of others."

Akin to chakras, Gurdjieff saw human beings as having three centers: physical, emotional, and intellectual. He observed "cosmic laws," such as the "Law of Seven." Also, he used symbols, frameworks such as the Enneagram, and physical exercises, including dances.

The Fourth Way: A Lucid Explanation of the Practical Side of G.I. Gurdjieff's Teachings by P. D. Ouspensky. Knoph, 1957.

Holotropic Breathwork

One can use breathing to induce an altered state of consciousness. In the 1970s, psychologist and medical doctor Stanislav Grof developed a simple, powerful technique called Holotropic Breathwork. He developed it after a shamanic experience and extensive cross-cultural research.

Dr. Grof states, "in the holotropic states, we can transcend the narrow boundaries of the body ego and reclaim our full identity." He points to an "inner wisdom" that we all possess to "work toward physical, mental, emotional, and spiritual healing, and developmental change." The practice prescribes deep, heavy breathing with the mouth open and eyes closed for at least an hour. Typically, within ten minutes, one's blood becomes highly oxygenated, and participants often report tingling and other sensations, tetany and twitching, visions that make sense of their lives, kundalini activation along the spine or from the solar plexus, and even being transported into an all-encompassing white light. A session usually includes music and "sitters" to watch over participants. His technique is not for people with vascular or cardiac problems and some participants may need therapeutic bodywork to ease "stuck" sensations.

It is remarkabe that simple, repetitive breathing can grant insights and healing so quickly. To no surprise, the practice also requires training and care to ensure a person can safely process a Holotropic experience. You can learn more at www.holotropic.com.

Tantric Buddhism

Buddhism views chakras somewhat differently than the Hindu and Sikh traditions that informed this book. Buddhism usually talks about four chakras, starting at the head and moving downward. It focuses on emptying oneself and results of spiritual practices.

In this tradition, ordinary people live in their head. Even when doing physical actions and feeling emotions, consciousness is mainly cognitive. Consider how, when you read, you don't explore all the strange squiggly shapes on the page. Rather, you "know" the squiggles stand for letters and words and you focus on their meaning. You say "I see" when you get the meaning, which feels real. But that is not true sight. It is mind-made meaning with practical benefits and many pitfalls. An initial goal of Buddhist chakra work is to quiet the busy interpretive mind with its many assumptions.

With practice, consciousness descends into lower chakras: the throat, heart, and navel. At the throat, we learn to communicate with thoughtful intent. Like words, our thoughts, perceptions, and feelings are maps and tools, not reality. This is a conscientious, mindful space. With more practice, we may learn to live from the heart with loving-kindness. Calm compassion guides us.

Those few who learn to live from the navel are like saints at one with the universe. They come to know the clear white light typical of *sahasrāra*. Perhaps ironically, each step further down into the body raises consciousness even as it simplifies, empties, illuminates, and liberates us.

Besides these traditions, there are psychological frameworks like the Enneagram and shamanic ceremonies that use substances like *ayahuasca* to promote a "higher self." The Enneagram focuses on ego defenses, emotional states, and the cultivation of virtue. It is beyond the scope of this book. The next section explores shamanism in more depth.

Entheogens: Medicines to Awaken

The term *entheogen* means "generating the Divine within." It includes any chemical substance, typically of plant origin, that is ingested to produce a non-ordinary state of consciousness in a religious, shamanic, or spiritual context. The result is often psychological and/or physical healing with possible insights. These are serious shamanic medicines.

Entheogens are *not* recreational drugs. They are non-addictive, may cause nausea, induce neural growth, are anti-microbial and anti-fungal, diffuse ego defenses, break bad habits and addictions, reveal and release psychological trauma, and highlight love and compassion. Entheogens are best understood as medicines that work well for participants with the right intentions in a healing context. Physical and mental preparation, a pleasant natural setting, a skilled and compassionate facilitator, and integration and after-care are all essential. Working with the mind is about molecules and meaning. Entheogens impact both. That is why they can grant luminous understanding, clear the past, motivate us toward new outcomes, and break or make habits that drugs, and talk, fail to address.

Shamanic substances may seem far removed from a yoga studio or chakra book. In practice, though, they are highly relevant. Most people are deeply stuck in their habits, identifications, narratives, and ways of perceiving and judging. They need spiritual electroshock therapy to get reacquainted with themselves and with existence to truly awaken maybe for the first time in their adult lives.

Readying Yourself

Not everyone starts out fit for a shamanic journey. Readiness is a person's ability to abide physical and emotional uncertainty and discomfort. It also refers to having tools to digest what emerges from highly altered states of consciousness. Entheogens work at the intersection of psychology, religion, and bungee jumping. Thus, activities like dream analysis, martial arts, meditation, poetry, yoga, and chakra work aid readiness. Comfort with allegories, interpreting metaphors, and capitalizing on extreme experiences for creative output also help.

A ready person trusts his or her unconscious enough to "let go." A ready person can focus away from the literal content of experiences toward the personal meaning of experiences. A ready person focuses on questions like, "What did I learn?" and "What might I do next?" Some standards and expectations of modern psychotherapy, such as maintenance of a pleasant "safe space," can hinder readiness. During a journey, a person may suffer a negative experience and extreme discomfort or confusion, which is apparently necessary for that person's awakening. Finally, ready persons understand that entheogens may re-open old issues and present new ones, taking one further away from practical successes in the world.

With readiness in mind, below you will find overviews of four common shamanic medicines with information about their safe use, typical results, and likely impact on chakra work. All the medicines and practices are legal in a number of places around the world, notably in Latin America.

* *The Ayahuasca Test Pilot's Handbook* by Chris Kilham. Evolver Editions, 2014.

Ayahuasca, Vine of the Soul*

This brackish drink is made from plant ingredients native to the Amazon rainforest. The term means "vine of the soul." Another term is *grandmother medicine*. It appears to mostly activate the 2nd and 6th chakras, though specific sessions may impact other chakras, often the heart chakra.

Typically, participants gather at night in a circle for 4 to 6 hours and drink 1 to 3 cups to induce a psychedelic effect that includes visions, sensations, internal dialogue, and such that lead to healing, insights, and growth. The second cup follows an hour after the first, with an optional third cup much later. The drink may cause some nausea and purging along with dizziness. A shaman goes beyond administering the drink to leading the group as a whole, and also goes around to work with each person to boost the drink's therapeutic impact. A ceremony often includes tribal or astral singing and music (drums, chimes, and guitars) to help set the mood and pace.

People tend to report different personalized experience in each session. An experience often includes amazing visuals in the mind's eye. A participant may also engage in a question-and-answer dialog with the plant (a part of his or her mind). The answers feel authentic as they bypass everyday convenient narratives or assumptions. The person may encounter various archetypes, from saints to spirit animals, including psychological entities like the *anima*. Over time, ego boundaries loosen, with each ceremony addressing new material that has been lying in wait just outside the ego's boundaries.

Ayahuasca's active ingredient is DMT. It is not for persons on SSRIs or MAOIs. It is legal for religious purposes in most of the Americas, including in the USA through the churches Santo Daime and União do Vegetal by Federal court ruling under the Religious Freedom Restoration Act.

Iboga, Release from Desire**

This psychedelic medicine is derived from an African root traditionally used in coming-of-age ceremonies by the Bwiti people of Africa and for the treatment of addiction, malaise, and sickness. Its active ingredient is ibogaine. It is a very powerful entheogen that realigns the whole chakra system.

Today, ibogaine is mainly used by clinics in Latin America to overcome substance abuse, notably heroin addiction. Compared to other treatment methods, it is quick and lasting with a 60% non-recidivism rate. It also has psychotherapeutic effects. It is more safely administered with a doctor's supervision and a heart monitor. It is a stimulant, but causes nausea, dryness, and ataxia. That is, a person suffers difficulty standing, walking, etc., and is confined to a bed for 8 to 12 hours.

When used for spiritual purposes rather than addiction treatment, *iboga*—the raw, unaltered plant—is preferred because it provides a far more stable experience.

Whatever the goal, this medicine has three phases: visionary, introspective, and integrative. The visionary phase has a dream-like quality but the person remains consciousness. The introspective phase has a therapeutic effect, helping the person conquer fears and negative emotions. The person often experiences instructive replays of life events. In the third phase, insights tend to follow in the days after.

This medicine is not advised for persons with heart conditions or psychiatric problems. Improper administration poses real danger. Sadly, in the USA, it is illegal and cannot be used to treat

** *Iboga: The Visionary Root of African Shamanism* by Vincent Ravalec, et al. Park Street Press, 2007.

addiction even though it is widely and legally used around the world with established medical centers and peer-reviewed research in Brazil, Costa Rica, Mexico, and New Zealand, among other nations.

Sapo, The God Molecule*

This medicine is a powerful psychedelic found in various Amazonian plants but is most plainly harvested from the poison glands of the Sonoran desert toad (*bufo alvarius*). Its active ingredient is 5-MeO-DMT, making it similar to *ayahuasca* but more potent. With proper dosage, it takes a person directly into the 7th chakra, as if the person has attained *samadhi*, total union with the Divine.

Sapo is usually given one person at a time in an intimate, safe, and natural setting. One method has a participant lie down with eyes closed. Another method starts with the participant standing up with eyes open. Dosage might be a single large dose to achieve "full release" quickly, or two or three graduated doses, to ease the person into the experience and with greater recall afterward. A gentle introduction can be important for people who lack experience with the 7th chakra. Whatever the method, onset is rapid (within 10 to 30 seconds) and lasts 5 to 20 minutes.

While affected, a person may appear to fall unconscious. Other effects include a powerful rushing or vibrating sensation, radical perspective shifting, immersive experiences with spiritual beings, loss of sense of time, muscle jerking and unusual vocalizations, tears of gratitude and joy, a feeling of unity with others and the Divine, communion in an all-encompassing white void, and a sense of consciousness without identity. Jung used strikingly similar language for the 7th chakra.

While emerging from *unio mystica*, a person gets reacquainted with him/herself and gains perspective on characteristics, beliefs, and such to either keep or discard. It is not for persons on SSRIs or MAOIs or vascular or cardiac problems. Sapo is legal in many Latin American countries, but not the USA.

San Pedro, Keys to Heaven**

Also called *huachuma* or *grandfather medicine*, this entheogen is derived from a common tall cactus in the Andes of South America, where it is drunk as a yellowish tea or greenish shake. Its active ingredient is mescaline. It has been in use for at least 3000 years (since 1300 BC).

Typically, participants sit in a circle with a shaman, enjoy tribal music, and drink 1 to 3 cups over the entire ceremony. Effects set in after an hour and last 10 to 14 hours. Participants usually feel some nausea but are able to eat fruit, nuts, and soup after several hours. Other effects include electric surges and shivers on the skin and throughout the body, slight dizziness, and a feeling of "crossed wires" and "permeable boundaries," similar to how many people feel awkward in their bodies and in social situations as teenagers. Giddiness and euphoria are possible, as are visual distortions. Persons and objects may appear stereotypical or geometric. The physiological mechanism is sympathetic arousal, especially in the peripheral nervous system. (In the brain, the right pre-frontal cortex gets active and beta waves are promoted.)

In older traditions, shamans subject participants to cold water, slapping sticks, and other harsh rite-of-passage activities. In contrast, modern traditions are often sedate, with participants

* *Tryptamine Palace: 5-MeO-DMT and the Sonoran Desert Toad* by James Oroc. Park Street Press, 2009.

quietly finding stillness in their thoughts and actions as they contemplate nature and the Divine. A ceremony may also include drumming, hiking, and bathing. Participants often report feeling highly connected and accepting of the world around them.

During this time, a participant may get in touch with any chakra—from a deep connection to the earth in the 1st chakra to the highest celestial realms in the 7th chakra. More importantly, he or she may have the chance to revisit past choices, even ones made early in life, and reconsider whether to choose differently. As a result, people also often report gaining a clear to-do action item or principle to make their lives better. The shaman must be on top of the experience, since participants can become animated, giddy, or agitated.

San Pedro, and its North American relative *peyote*, is legal in most of Latin American. In the United States, it is legal at the Federal level for religious usage but some states restrict or outlaw it.

Other naturally-occurring plant and animal medicines, including non-hallucinogenic ones such as *hapé*, *kambo*, and *sananga*, also assist with chakra work and promote healing, growth, and insights. They all complement yoga and meditation because cleaning the body is as important as cleaning up the rooms of your heart and mind. In fact, the ancient and sacred Hindu texts strongly suggest they used *soma*, an entheogen, to develop yoga in the first place.

• • • • •

Aftercare and Integration

After the use of entheogens, participants may wish to spend time—weeks, months, or years—grounding themselves with healthful physical activities such as exercise, gardening, meditation, and yoga. Cooking, dance, drawing, music, sculpting, singing, and writing can also help. The downtime helps people make sense of their experiences and integrate any insights and potential new habits into their daily life. These also give time to think twice about sensible choices regarding major life decisions such as changing homes, careers, or relationships. Rarely, a person may have an extreme lingering reaction. Perhaps prior assumptions are so shaken, or the release of blocked material so strong, that the person feels unmoored. This new sense of conscious awareness is strikingly at odds with one's whole lifestyle and philosophy. Nothing guarantees that growth is always pleasant!

In a few major cities and on the Internet, community services meet regularly in small groups or one-on-one to help people process their experiences and proceed with safety and satisfaction.

Shamanism and the Myers-Briggs Types: You may be familiar with this personality framework. All 16 Myers-Briggs types can benefit from shamanism, but specific types tend to handle such experiences more easily than others. In particular, all other factors being equal, the "NJ" and "SP" types (INFJ, INTJ, ENFJ, ENTJ, ISFP, ISTP, ESFP, and ESTP) report greater ease of benefit as they are tasked to make personal meaning of imagery from semi-conscious explorations while enduring intense physical hardship.

** *The Hummingbird's Journey to God* by Ross Heaven. O Books, 2009.

Preparation Before Ceremony
Here are key steps to consider before using entheogens for a spiritual journey.

1. Know your intentions: Consider topics to focus on or a desired outcome from the ceremony.

2. Keep *dieta*: Maintain healthy habits with fitness, food, and good company for three days to a week beforehand. Avoid negative interactions.

3. Read to inspire: Read a few pages on philosophy, psychology, religion, or a similar topic that will plant positive seeds in your unconscious. Avoid violent, sexualized, and similar negative media.

4. Review prior experiences: Review your most recent growth experience. Maybe you have kept a journal? Or sit in a quiet place, close your eyes, and review that experience as if you were there again.

5. Listen to your body: Where in your body do you feel numbness, pain, tightness, or other discomfort? Perhaps you have a serious health need. What chakra (or two) is closest to this spot?

6. Pick your friends: Whoever will facilitate or travel with you, ensure you all feel trust and respect.

7. Set the space: Like packing for travel, make sure you have your practical essentials and you are comfortable with the ceremony's location.

Integration After Ceremony
Here are key steps to consider after using entheogens to gain the most benefit.

8. What did you learn? What issues came up? Journal, voice record, or share with others. If you were to select a single take-home insight, what would that be?

9. What did you purge? Maybe you coughed or vomited? How did the experience help you remove a mask, de-program, or otherwise de-identify with or release something?

10. Which archetypes came up? You likely saw or even interacted with a mother, baby, sage, trickster, warrior, healer, plant, or animal. Briefly describe it. How did it appear and what did it say?

11. What chakras opened? Where did you feel the most sensation in your body? Typically, the 2nd and 6B chakras (near the gut and head) are most active. Anywhere else? How far did you activate kundalini energy? Did it rise from groin to crown, flood a specific chakra, or manifest another way?

12. Where have you gained greater connection? Did you gain a deeper, more honest connection with yourself, other people, the Other (your shadow), Nature, or the Divine?

13. How will you get grounded? How will you become more physically present and "solid" going forward? You might try cooking, dance, drawing, exercise, hiking, martial arts, sculpting, yoga, etc.

14. What is your next step? What single, small, spiritual action-step will you take today?

Part 4

More Jung

Here is a broad overview of Jung's understanding of the human psyche. You can locate your preferred psychological functions and adjust your chakra work accordingly. There are other key aspects of the psyche such as *ego*, *persona*, and *shadow*. In particular, Jung proposed a "Transcendent function" that arises naturally out of the tension of opposites within you. You can use techniques such as "active imagination" to encourage this function. The centerpiece is a view of the chakras as levels of psychological development.

Psyche as System

Early his career, Dr. Carl Jung observed a divide between conscious and unconscious activity in his patients and conducted word association experiments while corresponding with his colleague, Dr. Sigmund Freud. The results strongly supported the presence of psychological activity—mental and emotional—within a person's awareness and also outside of awareness.

Later, based on his years of hands-on work, Jung described eight psychological "types" in his book *Psychological Types**. First, he drew a distinction between an extraverted world of activity and an introverted one of reflection, and he observed that many people have a preference, coining the terms *extravert* (E) and *introvert* (I). A century of academic research by many psychologists supports this distinction. Keep in mind, these are *preferences*. Consider how we use both of our hands but one hand plays a dominant role. In the same way, we prefer introverting or extraverting. Consider this little activity:

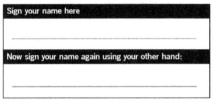

Notice how you can sign your name with both hands but using your preferred hand is easier, usually produces better results, and tends to be automatic.

Beyond a preference for Extraverting or Introverting, Jung observed four mental functions. They are broad ways of metabolizing experiences. These four functions are Sensing (S), iNtuiting (N), Thinking (T), and Feeling (F). Each person has one function as dominant. On the opposite page, you will find brief definitions and activities to help you understand the four functions. Consider which functions are easier or more fun for you. If the wording of a function doesn't make much sense, then it is likely not your preference! Of course, your upbringing, career, and a lifetime of growth can help you to explore and get skilled with all the functions to some extent even as you maintain a home-base. Thinking back to yourself as a teenager is a great way to sort your preferences.

The functions describe how we tend to operate as living beings. They are not easily measured surface traits. Jung hypothesized that they have resulted from eons of history. They reflect ways we have learned to balance the demands of many varied physical and social environments.

Finally, Jung observed that each of the four functions can express in an extraverted or introverted way. The result is eight "types," denoted here as two-letter pairs. For example, "Se" means Sensing that focuses on the external world while "Fi" means Feeling that focuses on one's inner world. The term "type" can be misleading, suggesting a box. Therefore, I use a modern term "cognitive process" instead. In the coming pages, you will have a chance to explore all eight cognitive processes.

* *Psychological Types: The Collected Works of C.G. Jung Vol. 6* by C. G. Jung. Princeton University Press, 1976.

The Four Jungian Functions

In the 1920s, Dr. Carl Jung described four ways we metabolize experiences. He called these "functions." Later, Isabel Briggs Myers popularized them starting in the 1940s. To locate your dominant function, <u>rank</u> the four sets below, with 1st as favorite, and put your top two in different rows.

Sensing (S)

Prefer to rely on the senses. Focus on tangible data and what is known, the present, and past experiences. Stay hands-on and act on practical options.

In the picture: *What details does this picture show? What experiences does it remind me of? What can I do with it?*

iNtuiting (N)

Prefer to rely on imagination. Focus on concepts, patterns, what's hidden, symbols, metaphors, and the future. Ask "what if?" and follow potential possibilities.

In the picture: *What is not apparent in the picture? What ideas does it spark to consider for the future? Is it symbolic or metaphorical?*

Thinking (T)

Prefer to rely on logic. Decide and organize based on objective criteria, deduction, models, measures, and impersonal, efficient principles.

In the picture: *What principles are at work? How can one define or measure what's shown here? Is the image accurate and efficient?*

Feeling (F)

Prefer to rely on values. Decide and organize based on social and interpersonal appropriateness, beliefs, and the importance or worth of oneself and others.

In the picture: *Does this speak to you? What's of value here? Who would like this image, and can we use it to help people?*

Chakra Work for All Psychological Types

Here are suggestions for chakra work based on which Jungian functions you most prefer.

People who prefer Sensing (S)...

Core: Rely on the senses. They focus on tangible data and what is known, the present, and past experiences. They stay hands-on and act on practical options.

Favorite Chakras: Often favor the 1st and 2nd chakras—that is, the root support and gut. These support concrete awareness and mobility. They tend to be grounded, aware of what's tangible and practical, and can be acutely in touch with their senses and body's reactions. Their consciousness is often focused on the environment and experiences they're having.

Challenges: Here are typical challenges to address. They may...

- Feel trapped in a common life with materialistic pursuits, stuck in a routine, and lacking curiosity beyond their local situation.
- Trust only what they know, favoring immediate tangible results. Find it hard to think outside the box or try new things.
- Be unaware of their true potential and under-estimate their own development. They may fear strange imagery, altered states, and "supernatural" experiences.

Practices: Prefer body-mind practices that promote physical fitness and bodily well-being. When feeling sluggish or tight, stretching and challenging workouts relieve a lot. They enjoy the moment and are motivated by results that improve appearance, flexibility, and energy. They benefit from practices that gently activate imagination and let them reflect on meanings.

People who prefer iNtuiting (N)...

Core: Rely on imagination. They focus on concepts, patterns, what's hidden, symbols, metaphor, and the future. They ask "what if?" and follow potential possibilities.

Favorite Chakras: Often favor the 6B and 7th chakras—that is, the third eye and crown chakras. These support abstract awareness and help them be imaginative, interpret almost anything, and have comfort with ambiguity and the unknown, archetypal images, potentials, and ideas. They are often aware of their own consciousness and how it changes.

Challenges: Here are typical challenges to address. They may...

- Live in their heads, ungrounded and disconnected from their body and the environment, missing important sensory feedback.
- Create fantasies and pursue a vision of how things could be regardless of facts on the ground, major obstacles, and practical costs.
- Over-estimate their own development and consciousness. They may be aware of potential, or imagine being a certain way, but still need to put in the actual work.

Practices: Prefer body-mind practices that utilize active imagination, dream-work, reading, and visualizing. They are motivated by anything that parts the curtain of reality to reveal exciting ideas and profound realizations. They benefit from slow breathing, craft activities to express meaning, nature hikes, and similar low-impact activities that ground them.

Where's Your Headstart? People are born with different talents, such as for music. In the same way, your favorite function gives you a headstart with some chakras. But you must still go through life to develop that potential, dealing with ego, exploring all the other chakras, and awakening.

People who prefer Feeling (F)...

Core: Organize and decide based on values, social and interpersonal appropriateness, beliefs, and the importance or worth of themselves and others, often with empathy and rapport.

Favorite Chakras: Often favor the 3rd and 4th chakras—that is, the solar plexus and heart. These support trust in one's feelings and identity, nurturing caring, and enjoying emotional intimacy. They tend to devote themselves to important causes, whether a person or job or ideology, and may invest a lot of energy, value, and meaning to "raise consciousness."

Challenges: Here are typical challenges to address. They may...

- Misplace trust in others or get caught up in a cause without checking facts, noticing consequences, or thinking things through.
- Take on other's pain as their own or forget their own needs to help others, perhaps to the point of codependency and harm.
- Over-estimate the worth of emotions or idealism, easily conned by slick talk—words that match their values—while projecting "unowned" negative feelings onto others.

Practices: Prefer practices that promote gratitude, forgiveness, loving-kindness, and peace to the heart. They are motivated by anything that positively impacts broken relationships and belief in themselves and others. They benefit from studying psychology, such as how they may be projecting, sublimating, and "othering" people in contradiction to their self-image.

People who prefer Thinking (T)...

Core: Organize and decide based on objective criteria, deduction, models, measures, and impersonal, efficient principles with attention to consistency of thought.

Favorite Chakras: Often favor the 5th and 6A chakras—that is, the throat and third eye. These support speech, reasoning out things, and visualizing how things work. They excel at problem-solving and applying mental power to figure out complex problems. They tend to objectify or define consciousness and may make a model of their development.

Challenges: Here are typical challenges to address. They may...

- Be stiff like a robot as they force their body past its healthy limits and keep a thick shell over their heart chakra to hide feelings.
- Come off as heartless and disconnected emotionally, criticizing themselves and others, and treating people as mere resources or objects to fix or deploy.
- Over-estimate the value of thinking, confusing intelligence for wisdom, or get caught up needing perfect logic or playing mind-games.

Practices: Prefer practices that are systematic and allow for an objective approach with stated reasons for things. They are motivated when they can efficiently reach their goals, with techniques for troubleshooting. They benefit from practices that gently expose and release repressed or confusing feelings and encourage appreciation and connection with people.

Eight Cognitive Processes

The four functions each manifest in two ways, extraverted and introverted, for eight processes total. This table presents them as pairs of "opposites" (left-right) that balance and synergize with each other.

Active Adapting
(Se: extraverted Sensing)
Immerse in the Present Context

Respond naturally to everything tangible you detect through your senses. Check what your gut instincts tell you. Test limits and take risks for big rewards.

Keen Foreseeing
(Ni: introverted iNtuiting)
Transform with a Higher Perspective

Withdraw from the world and focus your mind to receive an insight or realization. Check if synergy results. Try a realization to transform yourself or how you think.

Excited Brainstorming
(Ne: extraverted iNtuiting)
Explore the Emerging Patterns

Wonder about patterns of interaction across various situations. Check what hypotheses are most meaningful. Shift the dynamics of a situation and trust what emerges.

Cautious Protecting
(Si: introverted Sensing)
Stabilize with a Predictable Standard

Carefully compare a situation to the customary ways you've come to rely on. Check with past experiences. Stabilize the situation and invest for future security.

Timely Building
(Te: extraverted Thinking)
Measure and Construct for Progress

Make decisions objectively based on evidence and measures. Check whether things function properly. Apply procedures to control events and achieve goals.

Quiet Crusading
(Fi: introverted Feeling)
Stay True to Who You Really Are

Pay close attention to your personal identity and beliefs. Check with your conscience before you act. Choose behavior congruent with what is important to you.

Friendly Hosting
(Fe: extraverted Feeling)
Nurture Trust in Giving Relationships

Empathically respond to others' needs and values, and take on their needs as your own. Check for respect and trust. Give and receive support to grow closer to people.

Skillful Sleuthing
(Ti: introverted Thinking)
Gain Leverage Using a Framework

Study a situation from different angles and fit it to a theory, framework, or principle. Check this fit for accuracy. Use the leverage you gain to solve any problem.

* 8 Keys to Self-Leadership: From Awareness to Action by Dario Nardi. Radiance House (formerly Telos), 2005.

Finding Psychological Balance

Jung observed that people were happier and healthier when they are balanced. We benefit from specializing, yet we tend to become one-sided when we develop one cognitive process over all the others. To compensate, we can develop several more processes over a lifetime.

An able adult needs to both "perceive" and "decide" as well as operate in both the inner and outer worlds. Thus, minimally, we each rely on two processes: either Sensing or iNuiting to perceive plus either Thinking or Feeling to decide. Moreover, we use one process in an extraverted way and the other in an introverted way. For example, a person might prefer extraverted Intuiting (Ne) and introverted Feeling (Fi). Or a person might prefer introverted Sensing (Si) and extraverted Thinking (Te). These pairings minimally cover all the bases.

Now, please take a few minutes to explore the table at left. The goal is to locate which two cognitive processes best describe you at your core.

While exploring, focus on what has always come easily to you rather than what you have learned later in life or value or aspire to. Alternatively, if you shouldered a lot of pressure in your youth to be someone else, you may want to subtract out your community's and family's preferences. For example, American society encourages Timely Building for men, Friendly Hosting for women, and Cautious Protecting for everyone. When unsure, think back to your talents around age twenty. Or consider talking with someone who knows you well. You will likely spot a few possible fits.

Next, narrow down to your two best-fit processes. Specifically, select one process from the table's *top half* and a second from the *bottom half*. Also, be sure one process is from the *left column* and one is from the *right column*. Together, these two processes are your core, your home base, likely well developed by age twenty. Star these two.

If you wish, indicate one as dominant, taking a lead role, with the other in an auxiliary role.

Beyond two core processes, a person may develop further, particularly after midlife. Such processes tend to reflect one's opposite personality. For example, Ne-Fi and Si-Te are opposite pairings. Jung proposed that people may find balance by exploring and integrating aspects of their opposite. In the table, your opposites literally sit opposite of your core processes. Consider how using them can bring balance to your life and how you might develop them further. The next pages offer ideas.

By the way, we often learn to use various processes in limited circumstances, such as mainly at work, or to meet cultural demands, or to coordinate with our spouse.

The Eight Processes Form a Mandala: Psychological type historian Peter Geyer asserts that the functions are not a "model." That is, they are not meant as a dry scientific set of defined categories. Rather, they constitute a therapeutic framework*. We cannot measure them in a set way or limit them to specific people and eras. Rather, as I believe, they form a fractal-like *mandala* that we can keep revisiting and contemplating for discovery and growth. They are to the West what chakras are to the East.

* *"Type, Self and Personality"* by Peter Geyer, presented at the Ninth AusAPT National Conference, Sept 2010.

Snapshots of the Eight Processes

Active Adapting (Se)
Immerse in the Present Context

Act quickly and smoothly to handle whatever comes up in the moment. Excited by motion, action, and nature. Adept at physical multitasking with a video game-like mind primed for action. Often in touch with body sensations. Trust your senses and gut instincts. Bored when sitting with a mental/rote task. Good memory for relevant details. Tend to be relaxed, varying things a little and scanning the environment, until an urgent situation or exciting option pops up. Then you quickly get "in the zone" and use your whole mind to handle whatever is happening. Tend to test limits and take risks for big rewards. May be impatient to finish.

Excited Brainstorming (Ne)
Explore the Emerging Patterns

Perceive and play with ideas and relationships. Wonder about patterns of interaction across various situations. Keep up a high-energy mode that helps you notice and engage potential possibilities. Think analogically: Stimuli are springboards to generate inferences, analogies, metaphors, jokes, and more new ideas. Easily guess details. Adept at "what if?" scenarios, mirroring others, and even role-playing. Can shift a situation's dynamics and trust what emerges. Mental activity tends to feel chaotic, with many highs and lows at once, like an ever-changing "Christmas tree" of flashing lights. Often entertain multiple meanings at once. May find it hard to stay on-task.

Timely Building (Te)
Measure and Construct for Progress

Make decisions objectively based on measures and the evidence before you. Focus on word content, figures, clock units, and visual data. Find that "facts speak for themselves." Tend to check whether things are functioning properly. Can usually provide convincing, decisive explanations. Value time, and highly efficient at managing resources. Tend to utilize mental resources only when extra thinking is truly demanded. Otherwise, use what's at hand for a "good enough" result that works. Easily compartmentalize problems. Like to apply procedures to control events and achieve goals. May display high confidence even when wrong.

Friendly Hosting (Fe)
Nurture Trust in Giving Relationships

Evaluate and communicate values to build trust and enhance relationships. Like to promote social/interpersonal cohesion. Attend keenly to how others judge you. Quickly adjust your behavior for social harmony. Often rely on a favorite way to reason, with an emphasis on words. Prefer to stay positive, supportive, and optimistic. Empathically respond to others' needs and feelings, and may take on others' needs as your own. Need respect and trust. Easily embarrassed. Like using adjectives to convey values. Enjoy hosting. May hold back the true degree of your emotional response about morals/ethics, regarding talk as more effective. May try too hard to please.

What's This? These snapshots are based on brain research reported in *Neuroscience of Personality* by Dario Nardi, Radiance House, 2011. Explore here to clarify your strengths, blind spots, and imbalances.

Keen Foreseeing (Ni)
Transform with a Higher Perspective

Withdraw from the world and tap your whole mind to receive an insight. Can enter a brief trance to respond to a challenge, foresee the future, or answer a philosophical issue. Avoid specializing and rely instead on timely "ah-ha" moments or a holistic "Zen state" to tackle novel tasks, which may look like creative expertise. Manage your own mental processes and stay aware of where you are in an open-ended task. May use an action or symbol to focus. Sensitive to the unknown. Ruminate on ways to improve. Look for synergy. Might try out a realization to transform yourself or how you think. May over-rely on the unconscious.

Cautious Protecting (Si)
Stabilize with a Predictable Standard

Review and practice to specialize and meet group needs. Constant practice "burns in" how-to knowledge and helps build your storehouse. Specialization helps you reliably fill roles and tasks. Improve when following a role-model or example. Easily track where you are in a task. Often review the past and can relive events as if you are there again. Carefully compare a situation to the customary ways you've come to rely. In touch with body sensations. Strong memory for kinship and details. Rely on repetition. Check what's familiar, comforting, and useful. Tend to stabilize a situation and invest for future security. May over-rely on authority for guidance.

Quiet Crusading (Fi)
Stay True to Who You Really Are

Listen with your whole self to locate and support what's important. Often evaluate importance along a spectrum from love/like to dislike/hate. Patient and good at listening for identity, values, and what resonates, though may tune out when "done" listening. Value loyalty and belief in oneself and others. Attentive and curious for what is not said. Focus on word choice, voice tone, and facial expressions to detect intent. Check with your conscience before acting. Choose behavior congruent with what's important, your personal identity, and beliefs. Hard to embarrass. Can respond strongly to specific, high-value words or false data. May not utilize feedback.

Skillful Sleuthing (Ti)
Gain Leverage Using a Framework

Study a situation from different angles and fit it to a theory, framework, or principle. This often involves reasoning multiple ways to objectively and accurately analyze problems. Rely on complex/subtle logical reasoning. Adept at deductive thinking, defining and categorizing, weighing odds and risks, and/or naming and navigating. Notice points to apply leverage and subtle influence. Value consistency of thought. Can shut out the senses and "go deep" to think, and separate body from mind to become objective when arguing or analyzing. Tend to backtrack to clarify thoughts and withhold deciding in favor of thorough examination. May quickly stop listening.

The Jungian Psyche

Before we link the chakras to Jung's work, let's define some key concepts. The figure on the next page is a diagram of the psyche inspired by Jung's work. Mostly this is the psyche that you read about earlier as "Jung's 6th Chakra" (pages 56—61). A lot goes on there. Let's unpack it.

Absolute Unity: Outside everything, and yet suffusing all, is "Absolute Unity," the *unio mystica* that Jung describes for the 7th chakra. It is the center with the power of God and beyond comprehension.

Outer World: This is the universe we all share. It includes trees, libraries, brains, mountains, and a trillion other things, physical and cultural. As described for the 1st chakra, it is the *soil* we are born into. It includes elements that strongly influence us all, namely geography, family, peers, school, technology, media, our profession, and religion. These elements filter and influence us and also each other in a complex web. For example, media companies manufacture images and stories, broadcasting their own versions of the Outer World and how we can or should be.

You, the Big Circle: This is one person such as you or me. If life is an ocean, each of us is a tiny drop of water that reflects the ocean's essence as well as having our own unique Inner World. Notice that the upper half of the circle is solid while the lower half is permeable. In addition to the obvious ways the world influences us, it also quietly sets a stage for each of us unconsciously.

Persona: This is the set of social masks you wear in order to get along and be accepted. It is clothing style, job title, and all the habits that help you to get by in our Outer World, such as saying "thank you," not stealing, and waiting your turn in line. The persona also mediates your choice of career and marriage partner. The five arrows show the impact of the Outer World on you, via the persona. The way you tend to express your chakras with others is also here.

Your Ego and Personal Consciousness: This is the "I" or "me" you refer to as an independent, unique person with your own identity, memories, values, will, and self-estimation. It is your conscious mind. It is also home to your dominant function: Sensing, iNtuiting, Thinking or Feeling. The ego, by the way, has its own map of the psyche and of itself, though that map is often unconscious. When we learn about and reflect on human psychology and how people operate, we can compare that knowledge against our ego's map. For example, we might discover that our behavior doesn't align with our values or self-image. In this way, psychology can help us understand ourselves better.

The Unconscious: This is everything that is normally inaccessible to your conscious mind that you have excluded from awareness and self-definition. It strongly influences you and includes automatic activity as well as forgotten and suppressed material. It comes in two flavors: Your personal unconscious is material unique to you such as forgotten memories, while the Collective Unconscious is a repository of everything universally human, resulting from our biology and history as a species. The Unconscious is not a speculative concept. Early in Jung's career, he devised a scientific experiment to prove the unconscious exists by monitoring people's physiology during word association tests.

Absolute Unity (*unio mystica*)

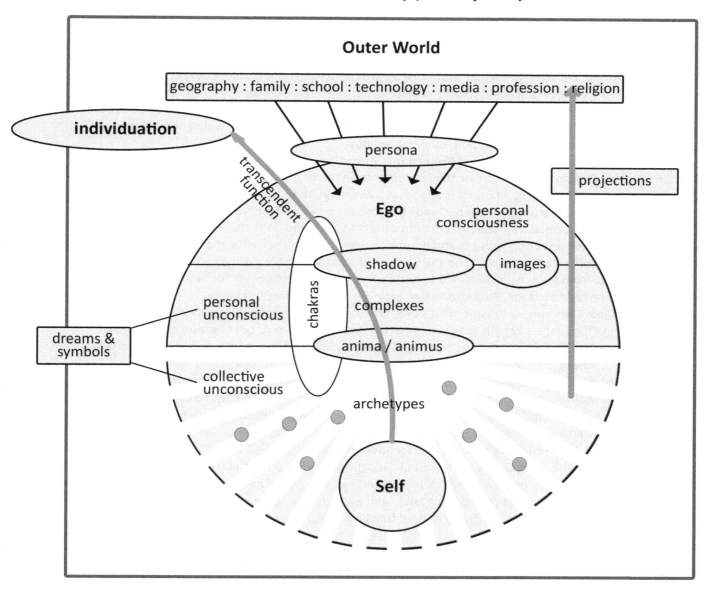

Figure 4: Major elements of C.G. Jung's framework of the psyche

* Adapted from Centro Jung de Buenos Aires—www.centrojung.com.ar © DanielWilhelm, 2008.

Complexes: A complex is an unconscious pattern of emotions, memories, perceptions, and wishes that is organized around a common theme such as power or status. You've likely heard of someone having an Inferiority Complex, Martyr Complex, or Messiah Complex. There are many more. They typically form by young adulthood and have a narrative quality. They influence how we interact with a category of person or group. For example, a man with the Don Juan (aka Player) complex experiences frustration and ignorance regarding women, and his playboy habits and beliefs keep up a history of superficial or heartbreaking relationships. Though we might say someone "has a complex," in actuality, complexes are troublesome when they rise up to *have us* in their grip. Uncovering and dealing with complexes takes introspection, feedback from others, willingness to change, and engagement with the shadow and *anima* or *animus*.

Shadow, Anima/Animus, and Projections: Your shadow is negative unconscious material that you project onto other people or things, demonizing them. It is all the stuff that resists inclusion in your persona. Keeping the material in shadow takes energy that distracts from other tasks and may show up as anxiety or depression. Oppositely, the *anima* (if male) or *animus* (if female) is positive unconscious material that you project onto others to exalt and deify them. The anima is a man's inner feminine self, a set of attributes and potentials akin to a women; while the animus is a woman's inner masculine self. Depending on the stage of life and level of maturity, these can manifest in different ways, from dreams and fetishes to a shift of personality in later life. Broadly, these link to your non-preferred functions. Projection often plays out through the 3rd chakra.

Images: These pop into your mind's eye, unbidden, during practices like meditation, yoga, or active imagination (page 122). An image might actually come as a voice or sensation or as a mix of all three. These images are more than creative ideas. They feel enticing, mysterious, and personally meaningful. Entheogens like *ayahuasca* greatly increase the flow of these images.

Archetypes, Dreams, and Symbols: The Collective Unconscious is home to archetypes such as Death, the Mother, the Trickster, and so forth. They are universal, appearing across cultures, and formed during our species' history. Dreams and symbols are ways we become aware of and represent archetypes and stay in touch with Absolute Unity outside the frame.

The Self, Individuation, and the Transcendent Function: The Self is the "true," unknowable you. Is it the seed you started as, with a DNA-like blueprint of your potential. The arrow out of it reflects a natural journey of growth, which Jung called *individuation*. The arrow starts in the unconscious and eventually breaks out of the big circle and even the big square, as spiritual growth. The mechanism of this growth is your Transcendent function, which we explore in the next section.

Chakras in the Jungian Psyche: Although Jung explored chakras, he did not explicitly integrate them into his framework of the psyche. If we take an extra step to place the chakras, we might place them in a way that intersects major elements. Chakras are both universal and personal in nature; they start out as unconscious, and by practicing yoga, using entheogens, or by other means, we "open" and align the chakras and everything they touch as we move upward into personal consciousness and beyond.

Your Transcendent Function

Besides the four Jungian functions, there is a so-called fifth function, or Transcendent function. What is this Transcendent function? In Volume 7 of the *Collected Works**, Dr. Jung defined the Transcendent function as "the process of coming to terms with the unconscious," and "a natural process, a manifestation of the energy that springs from the tension of opposites." When faced with conflict and one-sidedness, it helps us grow as we resolve that tension.

Beyond Personality Types

Earlier, we explored four mental functions and eight cognitive processes (aka types). Jung saw these as universally available to people and observed that each of us has a preference to operate in a certain way, such as having a dominant function. Later, American researcher Isabel Briggs Myers and others popularized Jung's idea as personality types. However, she did not include what Jung called the Transcendent function. Yet it is vital for our well-being. What is it?!

Contemporary Jungian scholar Steve Myers describes the Transcendent function as something we construct as uniquely ours. It may be obviously public and/or profoundly private, built from our life's joys and pains, actualizations and potentials, preferences and non-preferences. In "The Five Functions of Psychological Type," Steve Myers says a fifth function is essential—integral—to understand Jung's work:

"From the mid-1930s to the end of his life, Jung complained that most readers misunderstood the main point of his book *Psychological Types*. He viewed being a type as one-sided and problematic for a variety of reasons. His symbol-based solution to the 'type problem' involved developing a transcendent function to become the new dominant function of consciousness. However, this function has not featured in the popular use of his typology and Isabel Briggs Myers believed that the one-sidedness of Jung's eight types could be balanced by the auxiliary function. This has led to the transcendent function being widely ignored, and to a developmental philosophy that encourages a degree of one-sidedness."

Steve Myers proposes a solution. He says, "if we refer to Jung's typology as containing five functions not four, this more accurately represents both the content of the book *Psychological Types* and the primary value Jung saw in typology." Admittedly, this is easier said than done. As he also says, the construction of a Transcendent function "is difficult for people to grasp and they give up on it. That may be what happened with Isabel Briggs Myers—she thought she could never experience the Transcendent function. Yet she had one right under her nose—type theory. The theory that valued all types was itself an example of a transcendent function."

Isabel Briggs Myers contribution exemplifies how the Transcendent function works. As an Introvert with a dominant Feeling function, she did quite a bit of "Quiet Crusading." At the same time, she drew upon its opposite, extraverted Thinking, to add some "Timely Building." Her legacy integrated these opposites. She left behind an objective, validated psychometric tool and a resilient worldwide organization that promotes the value of individuals' gifts and talents.

* *Two Essays on Analytical Psychology* by C. G. Jung. Princeton University Press, 1972.

When Opposites Come Together*

How does this Transcendent function work? Firstly, it is how the psyche regulates itself. It gets active whenever two forces, urges, or ways of being within us come to oppose each other with equal strength. For example, a person may wish to stay true to his marriage vows, yet he also feels a strong drive for sexual exploration. Or a person values her current job security, yet she also yearns for freedom. Whatever the opposing forces, the person feels torn, suffers in odd ways, and may apply willpower to suppress it, which only stokes the fire. Life and psyche demand resolution in some form, for good or ill.

At the start, Jung explains, "there is full parity of the opposites" and "this necessarily leads to a suspension of the will, for the will can no longer operate when every motive has an equally strong counter-motive." Thus, we feel paralyzed to pick which road to go down. Moreover, "since life cannot tolerate a standstill, a damming up of vital energy results, and this would lead to an insupportable condition [unless] the tension of opposites produces a new, unity function that transcends them. This function arises quite naturally" and is "caused by the blockage." Sometimes we are unaware of the full scope of a conflict. For example, someone feels depressed and stuck and doesn't know why. In such cases, Jung advises dream analysis and active imagination (page 122), his favored therapeutic techniques, to give the conflict a conscious form.

Jung continues, "Once the unconscious content has been given form... the question arises as to how the ego will relate to this position, and how the ego and the unconscious are to come to terms. This is the second and more important step of the procedure, the bringing together of opposites for the production of a third: the transcendent function." He adds that the person must consciously make choices and changes to deal with the conflict. "At this stage it is no longer the unconscious that takes the lead, but the ego." Ideally, the ego is sufficiently strong and capable with resources to take wise action. Of course that is not always the case.

In the final phase, the Transcendent function offers an ingenious compromise, a synthesis of opposing forces. Jung explains, "there now emerges a new content, constellated by the thesis and antithesis, in equal measure and standing in a compensatory relation to both. It thus forms the middle ground on which the opposites can be united." For example, a man torn between marriage vows and sexual curiosity discovers a creative *sensuous* outlet. The outlet might be sexualized artistic expression, a reinvigorated sex life with his partner, or something else entirely. By this, the ego "finds in the middle ground its own counterpart, its sole and unique means of expression, and it eagerly seizes on this in order to be delivered from its division."

The Tension of Opposites is Your Fuel for Growth

The Transcendent function is more than a means to resolve inner conflicts. It generates the energy we need to grow psychologically. Imagine the push or pull between two magnets. Similarly, energy is generated from the give-and-take tensions that arise out of opposition and conflict. Of course, we may try to push away one side of the conflict. We may turn a blind eye to it. We may take it on but manage it badly. These poor responses invite neurosis or disaster. In contrast, with some guidance and practices like yoga, we can help the Transcendent function work its magic for us.

* From C. G. Jung's *Collected Works*, "Definitions" and "The Transcendent Function."

Please take a few minutes to reflect on your own gremlins. What opposing forces, urges, and aims churn within you? One or two may be pressing on the surface of your mind now. Just as often, an unresolved issue lurks quietly and seems to scurry out of sight the moment something brings it to mind. The following table may give you some ideas. Where is there tension?

Your daily routine vs. the lifestyle you daydream about.

Your current job position or career vs. a dream job or different career.

A current or past relationship difficulty, such as an unresolved breakup.

How you present yourself publicly vs. you by yourself, or how you feel while you are with others.

How your life has turned out vs. your potential and unrealized dreams.

Time spent caught in "either-or" / "us-them" drama versus compassion and detachment.

Female vs. male energies (in intimate relationships, and within yourself as *anima* or *animus*).

Confidence vs. self-doubt, shame, guilt, fear of success, or such.

Sensing vs. iNtuiting, and Thinking vs. Feeling.

How you feel around people who are significantly different than you.

Chakras that are closed or express in a negative way vs. being open and balanced.

Fulfilling vs. letting go of obligations to others.

Disturbing imagery from dreams, daydreams, or shamanic visions.

Anything you tend to avoid, particularly tasks that have lingered for years on your to-do list

Once you locate a tension, gently observe the feeling that comes up with it. That is, do you feel tense, excited, panicked, confused, angry, or what? The feeling is a source of energy for growth. The more energy you feel, the more meaningful it can be, and also the more challenging to transform. Artistic expression, chakra work, hypnotherapy, shamanism, yoga, and similar holistic techniques are all ways to approach transformation.

Transitions vs. Transcendence: Some theorists argue that there's no Transcendent function, only a transitioning function ("small t" versus "big T"). Perhaps those theorists haven't worked with kundalini or entheogens like *ayahuasca* and are unfamiliar with the rapid and tremendous transformations that are possible. Instead, they are used to talk-therapy and similar processes that work mostly with the 5th chakra at a slow pace, perhaps resulting on rare occasions in peak moments. When taking a slow path, this function's quiet work is only readily apparent after a long, diverse life. In contrast, we can get more proactive about growth—transcendence with a "big T." In particular, just as the lower chakras seem to concern themselves with progressive exploration of the four Jungian functions in all their attitudes and forms, the highest chakras are a natural workshop for exploring and leveraging the Transcendent function. Practices like yoga or shamanism that directly engage the crown chakra—pure consciousness without tensions or identity—greatly aid in the construction and expression of one's wholly unique self, one's Transcendent function.

Chakras as Developmental Levels

How does the Transcendent function relate to the chakras? The table at right treats chakras as levels of psychological development. We all start at birth in the 1st chakra. We move upward as we grow. The Transcendent function runs through all levels as our motor for growth.

This table packs in a lot of information. Mostly it describes which aspects of ourselves we tend to explore and when. For example, at Level 1, we rely on cultural and instinctual behaviors while we develop our dominant Jungian function. That would be Sensing, iNuiting, Thinking, or Feeling. Then much later, at Level 4, we enter into work and romantic relationships that complement our preferred functions. For example, if you prefer Sensing and Feeling, then you seek harmonious interactions with those who prefer iNtuiting and Thinking. Those relationships are cooperative and intimate rather than aggressive or projective, as they were in Level 3.

Here is a guideline: The chart divides into upper and lower halves. Broadly, in the lower half, we focus on developing our favorite functions as we learn to get by in the world, to employ our talents, prosper materially, and get along with others. This mostly occurs during life's first half, from birth to middle age. In contrast, in the chart's upper half, we explore everything else in the Jungian psyche. We may confront and work with our shadow, meet our *anima* or *animus*, and maybe grapple with a complex that has silently influenced us all along. This is mostly during life's second half. This phase may take us far—or not. It feels optional since it tends to not meet society's practical needs.

Now, what about the Transcendent function? It runs through every level. However, we are mostly unaware of its influence. We engage it obliquely in the 6th chakra. Only in the 7th chakra does it manifest directly to rapidly resolve issues. Since only a tiny minority of us spend time in higher chakras, the Transcendent function is usually unconscious and takes a lifetime to engage with it to build a unique self. Nonetheless, knowing steps to get to it and ways it manifests is a start.

As you trace your life's journey in the table and on the coming pages, keep several points in mind. First, tapping a chakra as a resource does not mean you are there developmentally. Ideally, you integrate lessons from lower chakras first. Second, society tends to push the 5th chakra, but many people are not there developmentally. Moreover, from early childhood, people hide the root and sacral chakras. They tend to keep private their sex life and emotional issues. Cognitively, we also tend to forget our origins. For example, we develop our dominant function in the lower levels. As adults, however, we take it for granted. While a toddler struggles to walk, the adult, barring disability, thinks nothing of it. As a result, many people are developmentally in a lower level but they are unconscious of their experience there and mistakenly identify with a higher level with which they only have passing familiarity. Third, keep your age in mind. Young people are usually in lower chakras and can tap a few resources above them. Fourth, you likely have an innate talent for a particular chakra, but you still need to earn your way to it. Fifth, do not confuse education, ideology, or position with development. An advanced education, broad-minded values, or a high social station may actually hinder growth. Finally, responding to the questions on the upcoming four pages will help you locate yourself.

Table 2: Chakras as Developmental Levels

Lvl	Name & Element	Themes	Psychological Development
7	**Crown** *sahasrāra* Light	Unity & Awakening	You **shed all identities**, the ego vanishes, and "you" enjoy fully unimpeded **pure consciousness**, linking "you" to the Divine and granting spiritual detachment, insight, and compassion. Directly work with **the Transcendent function**.
6B	**Third Eye** *ājñā* Ether	Psyche & Imagination	You create your own meanings and identity as you **play with the many ways you might be**, **exploring all functions, especially the shadow functions,** and archetypal manifestations. Can be disorienting, insightful, or manipulative.
6A	**Third Eye** *ājñā* Metal	Vision & Systems	You **actively develop your ego** with new habits to be more sophisticated and aligned to the world as it actually is. You **improve perception and decision-making** toward a life purpose. Can be virtuous, prideful, or tyrannical.
5	**Throat** *vishuddha* Air	Speech & Reason	You **observe, assess, and question your ego pattern** and your own and others' behavior. You aim to **self-develop, mindful to include your opposite**. Can be self-critical.
4	**Heart** *anāhata* Wood	Balance & Empathy	You attend to a **humanistic conscience** and commit to moderating activities and **cooperative relationships that complement your preferred functions** while gently growing with your opposite. Can feel vulnerable as you show love.
3	**Solar Plexus** *manipūra* Fire	Action & Projection	You stick to your ego pattern, typically your **dominant and auxiliary functions**. You may easily idealize, ignore, or vilify what differs from your ego, such as your shadow side. Develop **willpower**. Can be **empowering or extreme with a cause**.
2	**Sacrum** *svādhishthāna* Water	Danger & Renewal	You rely on your **dominant function** to meet your **needs** and manage life's conflicts and options. Slowly develop an **auxiliary function**. Collect baggage. Can be **self-conscious**.
1	**Root** *mūlādhāra* Earth	Soil & Seed	While **developing your dominant function**, you absorb and rely on cultural norms and routines, often for generic survival activities such as eating. You are **impressionable**.

LEVEL 1

Root: Soil & Seed
you exist, you have potential

You absorb and rely on cultural norms and routines, often for generic survival activities such as eating. Meanwhile, you slowly **develop your dominant function**. You are **impressionable**. Having a loving parental figure is key for healthy development here.

Where do you feel most comfortable?

What are the top three values you share with your culture?

Which cognitive process/es* does your culture favor most?

When do you feel most free to explore nature?

When you feel deprived, how do you react?

LEVEL 2

Sacrum: Danger & Renewal
you feel, you adjust and explore

You rely on your **dominant function** to meet your **needs** and manage life's conflicts and options. Slowly develop an **auxiliary function**. Collect baggage. Can be **self-conscious**. Having a suitable role-model and room to explore are key for growth.

What is your main talent?

What is the mask you wear for which people know you best?

What are your top two best-fit cognitive processes*?

When do you feel most free to be affectionate (or physically intimate)?

How do you respond when feeling shame?

* Page 104 summarizes the eight Jungian cognitive processes.

LEVEL 3

Solar Plexus: Action & Projection
you struggle, you act with confidence

You stick to your ego pattern, typically your **dominant and auxiliary functions**. You may easily idealize, ignore, or vilify what differs from your ego, such as your shadow side. Develop **willpower**. Can be **empowering or extreme with a cause**. Friends and community are now key.

What is your truth?

Who do you tend to idolize, respect, dislike, and vilify?

When are you most confident to take action?

When do you feel most free to admit your failings?

What enrages you, and why?

LEVEL 4

Heart: Balance & Empathy
you love, you make yourself vulnerable

You attend to a **humanistic conscience** and commit to moderating activities and **cooperative relationships that complement your preferred functions** while gently growing with your opposite. Can feel vulnerable as you show love. Having a spouse and children are key.

Who delights you?

Who complements or completes you, and what are that person's likely cognitive processes*?

Who has your total and everlasting commitment of love?

When do you feel most free to be vulnerable?

What great loss do you still grieve over?

LEVEL 5

Throat: Speech & Reason
you speak, you gain perspectives

You **observe, assess, and question your ego pattern** and your own and others' behavior. You aim to **self-develop, mindful to include your opposite**. Can be self-critical. Having an audience, customers, or clients, plus colleagues and a boss or a coach are key.

How do you build rapport?

On what topics are you most qualified to speak (or write)?

What scientific or philosophical aid do you rely on to examine and fix your own behavior?

When do you feel most free to hear and implement others' advice?

How do you respond when someone lies to you?

LEVEL 6A

Third Eye: Vision & Systems
you observe, you understand how it all works

You **actively develop your ego** with new habits to be more sophisticated and aligned to the world as it actually is. You **improve perception and decision-making** toward a life purpose. Can be virtuous, prideful, or tyrannical. Having employees or similar persons in your charge is key.

How do you lead people different than you?

What are the core principles of your problem-solving process as a professional?

How do you sort between reality, wishful thinking, and illusions?

When do you feel most free to reach out and work with opponents?

How do you cope when feeling overwhelmed?

* Page 104 summarizes the eight Jungian cognitive processes.

LEVEL 6B

Inward Third Eye: Psyche & Imagination
you dream, you learn from the unconscious

You create your own meanings and identity as you **play with the many ways you might be, exploring all functions, especially the shadow functions,** and archetypal manifestations. Can be disorienting, insightful, or manipulative. May face tricksters. Having a protégé is key.

When do you trust your unconscious?

Which cognitive process/es* do you pretty much reject?

What is your totally unique and meaningfully creative contribution to the world?

When you do feel most free to laugh at yourself?

How do you react to chaos and insanity?

LEVEL 7

Crown: Unity & Awakening
you evolve, you connect back to the Divine

You **shed all identities**, the ego vanishes, and "you" enjoy fully unimpeded **pure consciousness**, linking "you" to the Divine and granting spiritual detachment, insight, and compassion. Directly work with **the Transcendent function**. May face your demons. Having a Deity is key.

What is the meaning of death?

Of your top three values, which one are you willing to give up?

What is your spiritual practice to negate your ego and reconnect with the Divine?

When do you feel most free to embrace a great fear?

How do you pass on your life's wisdom?

Your Developmental Journey

Now that you've explored the chakras as developmental levels, you may have a clearer idea of your challenges, life lessons, and the roles of other people in your life. Here are some suggestions to help you further refine your understanding.

First, selecting your current level is not so important. Dr. Jung did not propose a strict model of developmental levels. Nor did he aim to place anyone into a box, though he left us with some terms and guidelines. As typical for him, the chakra levels are concepts. Exploring these concepts may likely lead to several possible interpretations. The act of exploring by itself can lead to insights. You need only reflect on and personalize the concepts to your own life. Of course, a particular level or interpretation may speak quite strongly to you, which is fine.

Second, consider that there are many ways to visualize development. One way is a linear staircase. Using that metaphor, you climb up a set of steps with plateaus between the jumps. Or maybe the levels are windows of opportunity. Each window tends to open at certain times, and you want to take advantage of those; otherwise, you miss out and grow stale and frustrated later in life. Or perhaps a more appealing metaphor is a spiral. You start small and tight at the spiral's center. As you spiral outward, you encounter new challenges and also revisit old ones from a fresh perspective. Thus, you repeatedly encounter certain themes over a lifetime.

More in line with kundalini yoga, imagine a field of pure vibrating consciousness. Within that field, the seed of *you* starts to grow. Your ego first works like a tiny cell. The cell's boundaries both define it and restrict what enters and exits. Quickly, the cell divides and is more "concrete" than the field around it. With time, its mass multiplies and organizes to form a full organism—the adult you—made up of many cells with limbs, senses, thoughts, feelings, and so forth. You maintain boundaries and adopt various masks, props, and lines. On occasion, you look in a mirror and observe yourself, "get real," and make adjustments. That's when you shift to toughen, soften, improve, or remove aspects of yourself. A whole change of story may be in order. If you are like most people, you rarely awaken to your true nature. In those moments when you do, you reconnect with the ambient field of consciousness. In the chakra tradition, this awakening is like a lotus flower suddenly opening to reveal its full beauty. Alas, after an awakening, you may easily fall into the vortex of a particular chakra, again forgetting your true nature, where the lotus is but a dream. Ultimately, at the end of your lifecycle—or whenever your body expires—you rejoin that great field of consciousness. The end's details are unknown. Perhaps like a field of wheat, we are harvested for something greater. Or we dissipate into nothing at all or meet some other fate or destiny. The graphic at right, with its three-and-one-half kundalini loops, represents this process. Start at the bottom, follow the arrows, and loop around toward the top.

What about the Transcendent function? Whatever your development looks like, you have options to awaken and stay awake. The process involves learning and emptying, hurting and healing, activating and grounding, among a myriad of polarities. The coming pages offer techniques you can use to tap these tensions of opposites within you, to keep fueling your journey.

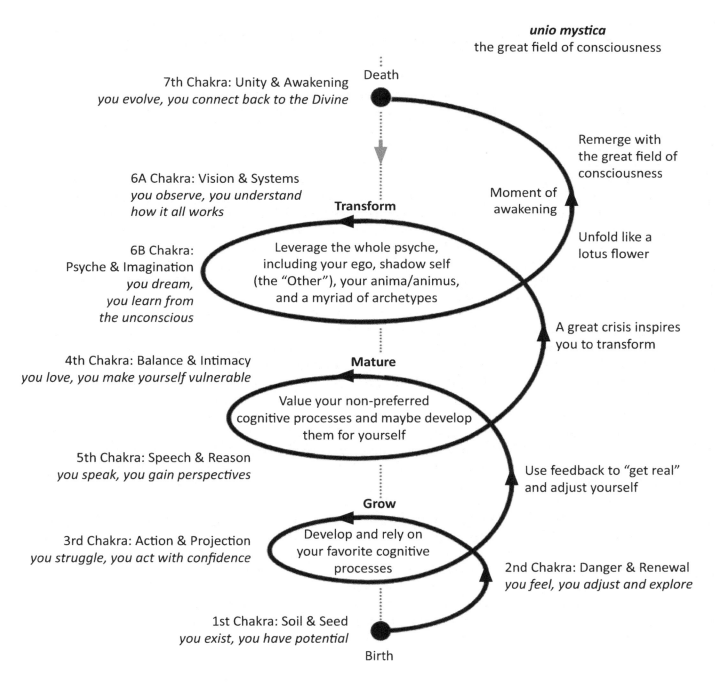

Figure 5: The *Jung on Yoga* spiral of development

Active Imagination & Jung's 6th Chakra

Just as the Jungian functions are comparable to the chakras, and the Transcendent function relates to awakening, so too does Jung offer a practice—active imagination—as his answer to kundalini yoga. It engages the 6th (6B) chakra and blends Western and Eastern traditions.

What is active imagination? In brief, you relax into a creative state to engage in dialog with your unconscious. You might draw, paint, sculpt or write; or you might simply sit and contemplate an image such as a painting. Any visual stimulus such as a religious symbol, tarot card, or even an advertisement may do. Jung says*: "The point is that you start with any image... Contemplate it and carefully observe how the picture begins to unfold or to change. Don't try to make it into something, just do nothing but observe what its spontaneous changes are. Any mental picture you contemplate in this way will sooner or later change through a spontaneous association that causes a slight alteration of the picture. You must carefully avoid impatient jumping from one subject to another. Hold fast to the one image you have chosen and wait until it changes by itself. Note all these changes and eventually step into the picture yourself, and if it is a speaking figure at all then say what you have to say to that figure and listen to what he or she has to say."

The goal is not to edit or critique the image to make it better or more interesting. Nor are you brainstorming or engaging in free association. Instead, let the image "come alive" on its own. When it does, it might be absurd, childish, obscene, or scary. That's okay. Let the image continue to animate and tell its story. When you feel ready, you may ask it a question. Note its response like a patient parent listening to a child describe fantasy play. After entertaining this state, journal the interaction as-is without embellishment or shame. As you record the experience in words and sketches, and likely as you reread it later, meanings that link to your life may emerge. Over time, as you keep up this practice, themes will surface as well as possible solutions to polarities.

Consider an example. Let's say you focus on a parked car in a parking lot. Its sleek black styling or familiarity from childhood catches your eye. You keep your mind clear as you keep focusing on it. Suddenly, you "notice" (imagine) a bird trapped in the car. You note the bird's color and demeanor. From there, allow it to act. Maybe it sings, flutters about, hits against the window, speaks to you, or catches fire. Then you ask it, "Do you have a message for me?" It answers in your voice, "Let me free!" Of course this comes from your own mind, but seems unbidden and creative.

Active imagination requires intense focus, which takes effort. You aim to engage the 6th chakra as described by Jung (pages 56-61)—the space of psyche and imagination. You allow a give-and-take between muses (the unconscious) and your practical, sober, conscious self. This method works notably well in the wee hours, when listening to music, after exertion, or when feeling tormented by an emotional situation. Ideally, the object draws your interest already. It has an "energy" or is mysterious. Finding what works well for you is part of this practice. Over time, active imagination facilitates transitions ("small t") and may lead to a transcendent experience ("big T").

* *C.G. Jung Letters 1906-1950*, Gerhard Adler, Editor. Routledge and Kegan Paul: London, 1973, page. 460.

Working with Opposites

Both Jung and yoga help us see imbalances and tensions in our lives. A chakra, function, or other aspect of ourselves can express in a healthy or unhealthy way. There are so many ways to be in flow or out of sorts! Fortunately, we can rebalance using a simple yet powerful technique.

Often, imbalance results when we have an unmet need and try to fill that need in a quick, reactive, or superficial way. That is, we try to protect ourselves, avoid pain, or fill a void. Over time, reactions become habits. We may even unconsciously copy a habit from our parents, friends or media. Whatever the source, a behavior may become so habitual that we don't notice it until someone points it out and it noticeably hinders our lives. Even then, circumstances may make change a challenge as adults. We may feel caught in a web of obligations and routines. Fortunately, we can start to rebalance in seven steps.

1. First, locate an imbalance. Reflect on how you operate, and nominate an area to work with. Sometimes you know right away. Other times, you may have pushed it out of your mind; so ask a friend for feedback. Just noticing, naming, and admitting an unhealthy habit is a great start.

2. Next, find a quiet space and do two minutes of stretching, deep breathing, chanting, prayer or such to relax your body and mind. End with thirty seconds of stillness and a blank mind.

3. When ready, sit tall and hold out your hands, palms up and open.

4. In your left palm*, "place" the unhealthy behavior. You might hold a literal object, photo or such that represents it. With eyes closed, visualize doing that behavior. Feel what that is like. Dwell on it. Then ask, "What need is it meeting?" Listen quietly to hear or see an answer.

5. Now, in your right hand*, do the same with a healthier, balanced behavior. You may hold a literal object to represent it. With eyes closed, visualize a time when doing that behavior felt great, even if that has not happened much before or in a while. Feel what it is like. Then ask, "What need am I meeting here?" Listen quietly to hear or see an answer.

6a. When needs are similar, ask the left hand (the unhealthy side) if it is okay to do the healthy behavior (in the right hand) a little more often, perhaps as an experiment. Wait for an answer. If you hear "yes," great. If you hear "no" or uncertainty, ask, "Please tell me more," or "What might make it easier to get your permission?" Allow your mind to show or tell you something. You are done with this step when you get permission.

6b. When the needs differ, focus on the left hand, clear your mind, and ask for other ways you might meet that need. This is not brainstorming. Rather, wait patiently to receive some kind of image or words. If the process is less than satisfying, do some deep breathing and stretching again with your eyes closed for two minutes, then try again. You can also move to a different location and/or set up two chairs, to your left and right, and move between the chairs as you speak with each side of yourself. Alternatively, put the issue on the "back burner" and try again later.

7. To wrap up, give thanks to each part of yourself and shake out your hands. Consider writing the key lesson on a post-it note to put on a mirror or refrigerator as a gentle daily reminder.

* Feel free to reverse the hands if you are left-handed.

Western & Eastern Traditions

Akin to yin and yang, there are two general ways to work with the Transcendent function.

Western: Ego Development

Popular Western models such as Spiral Dynamics usually present stages of development. They focus on a conscious, linear, upward climb of psycho-social progress over a lifespan or the span of human history. Models that are tailored to Jung's psychological framework also tend to focus on ego development.

This approach focuses on making the ego more sophisticated, such as learning how to perspective shift to others' points of view. These models act as a lens, language, and lever for change, and are practical for improving quality of work and relationships in the world. These models are easy to present in a seminar or through a book, though one must be diplomatic in helping people locate what stage they are in versus where they perceive themselves.

Ego development makes sense for many applications. After all, ego manages the boundary between the conscious and unconscious, so why not improve it? However, this approach also tends to be cognitive and behavioral, with consciousness located in the head and accessed through words, and it tends to focus on how to conform the person to the aspirations of modern liberal society even when framed as personal growth. Past societal norms and alternative viewpoints are typically categorized as lower stages. Moreover, people can simply mimic pre-scribed words and ideas and end up with false consciousness, relying on labels and yet out-of-touch with their timeless core humanity.

Eastern: Ego Dissolution

Chakra work is an example of an Eastern approach that focuses on ego dissolution. The focus is on experiential practices, not models. Practices often involve the whole body, such as through meditation and yoga. Progress is experienced as "opening up," greater flexibility, and the cultivation of simplicity and compassion.

Ego dissolution focuses on stripping away armors, blinders, blockages, and other layers of ego that suppress the pure shining consciousness that already exists within each and all of us. Practices like kundalini yoga focus on helping a person bring a free flow back to body, mind, and spirit. These practices take space and time. They utilize breathwork, stretching, release of trauma stored in the body, eating healthy, quieting the mind, and simplifying life.

This approach is holistic. It locates consciousness throughout and around the body. Ego, no matter how developed, is a costume and set of lines and props, like in a stage play. Or it is like a curtain that separates people from themselves and others. Simply parting it aside can have a powerful impact. Jung recognized this approach as deeply psychological and he was impressed with kundalini as a means for change. That said, this approach has pitfalls. A person may over-react to early progress in his or her practices, find "staying awake" in a materialistic world a great challenge, or find freedom but not be ready with the knowledge and skills needed for practical work in the world.

Part 5

What's Next?

We enter the home stretch of our journey. Most of us face some big, practical obstacles in our present world. Fortunately, there are four concrete steps you can take today. We wrap up with the Wheel of Conscious Experience. Use this tool to locate where you currently are in your journey of life and what spaces you will likely head into next. Like the seasons, the Wheel turns from transformation to flow to conflict to suffering, and around again. Finally, you will find a list of references for further in-depth reading.

Today's Challenges

People who have awakening experiences often report similar impressions when reflecting on life in the ordinary world. During a powerful non-ordinary state, we drop our barriers. Filters vanish. Baggage melts away. What we already know to be true gets a spotlight. Priorities shift. Afterward, we return to our daily lives already in progress. Daily life is usually busy and full of conflicts. It is saturated with media messages, strained relationships, and financial demands. "Staying awake" is tough. We may feel lonely, and implementing new priorities is often a practical challenge. This little book offers a framework—the timeless treasures of Jung and yoga—to face those challenges. Besides those, here are three key observations people tend to share after a transformational experience.

Peace: After ten minutes of deep breathing, most people feel relaxed. Even more so after a long yoga session, *ayahuasca* ceremony, or such. For those participants, deep issues often come up followed by tremendous relief. Anger, anxiety, depression, disgust, fear, guilt, pride, shame—they look honestly at the origin of these and then let them go. The result is balance, room to live freely, and a gentle invitation to live more responsibly. In contrast, media reports endless conflict in tones of helplessness and shock. We are taught to suppress or weaponize our issues. Workplaces can be contentious. The main take-away lesson is that peace with others comes from peace on the inside.

Connection: What brings inner peace? In one form or another, people tend to report a tragic lack of connection. They feel disconnected from others, themselves, Nature, and/or the Divine. Tiny, fleeting bursts of text and photos cannot replace authentic in-person sharing. Similarly, modern society shames people to not even *think* the word "God." What then fills our innate spiritual needs? Everywhere, "Truth" is crafted, labeled, positioned, and assigned value with a purpose. That purpose is usually profit or power, like teams competing for trophies. Even spirituality gets packaged. Signaling one's virtue to be socially well-branded and feel like a better person is called *spiritual materialism*.

Truth: Maybe we live in a "Matrix." That is, the world can feel like a grand stage play or multi-player video game, where each of us is wearing a mask (or three), using props, and playing parts. Alas, most of us tend to forget we are at play. Of course, we share a definite material world with tangible consequences. Ideally, we make choices and utilize our talents to leave a more pleasant and profound stage for others after us. Nonetheless, at best, the world is a classroom with distractions. Many people who have a major awakening experience are struck by life's fictional nature. It is *maya*. Yet, apparently, we are tasked to play a part and called to play honestly and at our best.

With challenges like these, you may wonder how anyone can possibly stay awake? To start, on the next page are four steps you can take today to make this book more practical in your own life. Afterward, you will find The Wheel of Conscious Experience. It is based on hearing many people's transformational and *numinous* experiences. When you are sucked into a particular state, you can locate and name it (or an approximation of it) on the Wheel. Then you may shift to a better state. You will also find diagrams and brief explanations of the Wheel's quadrants.

Whatever your next steps, may you enjoy health, happiness, and holiness.

Your Next Steps

You cannot direct your spiritual journey, but you can take steps to make the most of it. A gardener can till soil, plant seeds, and apply a balance of water and sunshine. Similarly, you too can nurture your development. Here are four steps you can take starting today.

1. Start a body-mind practice. You might try meditation, yoga, martial arts, or entheogens. Whatever attracts you, focus on breathwork, balance, and moving your energy. Conscious breathing is a gateway to greater awareness of your whole nervous system. Regular practice, daily or even just weekly, will help your psyche loosen up and function in a more harmonious way. Stress will lessen. Psychological defenses will soften. You will find yourself re-energized and also calmer. If you prefer to start at home, try some of the kundalini exercises on page 77, or follow along with a manual or an Internet video, or find a local class.

2. Notice how you operate. With this guidebook, you may start to notice when you get caught up in the vortex of a particular chakra in healthy and unhealthy ways. For example, the 3rd chakra (solar plexus) can be a space of confident action or a space of projection and fanaticism. Often, the unhealthy space feels exciting or familiar. It feeds the ego, or at least is a temporary refuge. It is useful to notice your triggers and response patterns in order to sidestep chakra traps and stay compassionate when you and others get stuck in a chakra. In time, you will get a sense of which chakras need more attention. You might do the same with the Jungian functions.

3. Try the mindful activities for each chakra. At a minimum, once weekly, try a different activity. You might set aside an hour or pledge yourself to try out a small change over the course of the week, such as listening more objectively. Ideally, start with the 1st chakra and work your way in order up to the 7th. A particular chakra's issues may beg for attention. Besides the activities here, the Internet and chakra books offer many more activities. Alternatively, set aside free time for people and activities that differ from habit and comfort. Whatever you try, it is important to actually do something in addition to reading if you want to see changes.

4. Attend to the unconscious. By its nature, the unconscious lies outside of your awareness. To help expose and integrate its content into your life, consider keeping a journal of dreams and transcendent experiences. Compile your own "Red Book," which is a record of Dr. Jung's dreams and visions. Or attend more to symbols, maybe creating your own or locating icons and artwork, such as *mandalas*, that represent challenges and aspirations. You needn't force it; merely let these accumulate. Jung would also encourage you to take advantage of coincidences, or *synchronicities*. He coined this term. It refers to a personally meaningful confluence of events.

The Wheel of Conscious Experience

The graphic at right is a great wheel with many spokes. It shows states of consciousness and how they relate. You can use it to name where you tend to "go" psychologically in particular situations. You can also use it as a guide to pinpoint where you might "shift" to respond to situations more effectively, typically moving clockwise. If some spokes look unfamiliar at first blush, you might brainstorm times when you have visited those in the past and how you got there.

The wheel is organized along two axes. The horizontal axis is "alertness." Unconscious deep sleep sits on the far left while, oppositely, a super-changed task focus sits on the far right. The vertical axis is "maturity." More elevated states such as loving-kindness sit toward the top, while more bestial, negative states such as rage sit at the bottom of the wheel. The many other spokes reflect common shades of conscious experience. They are like variations on a color wheel.

The wheel divides into four quadrants, or seasons, as summarized here.

	Left Side (lower energy/inner focus)	Right side (higher energy/outer focus)
Top of Wheel	**Transform (winter)**: Trust the unconscious for growth, healing, and insights.	**Flow (spring)**: Explore the world in creative ways and share wisdom.
Bottom of Wheel	**Suffer (fall)**: Stuck in a rut or web of old behaviors, routines, and substances.	**Conflict (summer)**: Use force, tricks, and defenses to build up ego and push goals.

All four quadrants are useful and needed. Each is home to a key activity for spiritual transformation. Consider how the full passage of seasons is necessary for the cycle of life. Or, to use a Jungian metaphor, transformation is like alchemy, which requires a mix of heating, filtering, combining, and cooling. Whatever the metaphor, while we might wish to say in the wheel's top half, we are human.

You likely have favorite spokes. They come from life experiences and cultural influences. For example, in American society, capitalism and democracy encourage ego conflicts in the lower-right quadrant. Fortunately, vibrant give-and-take may also advance us to the wheel's upper half. Whatever the roots, favorites arise from habit: repeatedly taking the same paths, often starting in childhood. Where you focus your attention, the emotions and thoughts you entertain, the actions you take—these impact all the chakras to "lock in" good or bad habits. In Sanskrit, these habits are called *samskaras*. Often, we are unconscious to the *samskaras* that tether us to particular spokes.

Now find one spoke you tend to fall into more than you like. Consider, from past experience, the people, locations, and situations that tend to draw you into it; then brainstorm ways to prepare, slow down, or step away. Your goal is to move to an adjacent spoke above it. Think of that new spoke as an alternative way to respond. Think of when and how you've gone there before. With practice, you can also visit the center of the Wheel and shift to anywhere. Yet another option is "shock therapy." Entheogens like *ayahuasca* can quickly move to higher spokes and help us make the most of them.

To work with the Wheel, let's dig deeper....

* See the 7th chakra (pages 62-67) and the Jungian psyche (pages 108-110) regarding **unio mystica**.

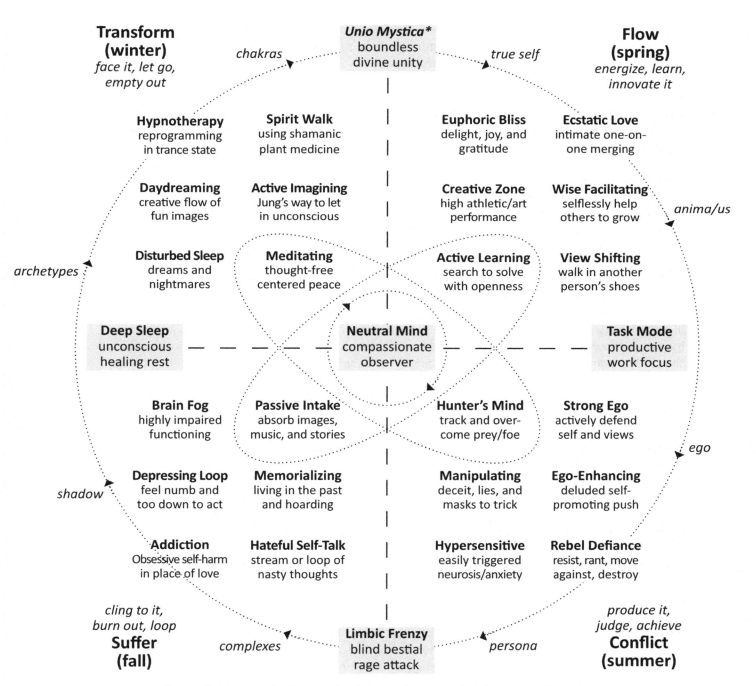

Figure 6: Major polarities and points on the Wheel of Conscious Experience

First, notice the arrows on the Wheel. They go clockwise. Wherever you are, you can move forward toward new spokes, eventually entering a new quadrant and going all around the Wheel. This is like flowing with the seasons, year after year.

You may wonder, can you go against the flow, counter-clockwise, or jump around the Wheel? Yes and no. Certainly you can shift to adjacent spokes. Otherwise, far jumps are like tackling a steep incline. For example, if you are in Task Mode, you are quite busy, focused, and productive. Can you shift into Active Learner or the Creative Zone? Yes! Can you move into Daydreaming? (Who hasn't, while supposedly working?!) Well, we daydream when we tire of a task or when something else weighs on us. So really, you either move around for a change of environment or you tire yourself out before making such a big jump.

There is a secret shortcut between spokes. At the Wheel's center is the Neutral Mind. This is a Buddhist concept. With a neutral mind, we are alert and calm, detached yet compassionate. It is like walking through the woods and noting the trees and stones, evaluating them without judging them or feeding a strong reaction. When you practice entering this space, you can use it as your shortcut to go anywhere on the Wheel at any time.

Spokes located in exactly opposite spots on the Wheel are polarities. They mirror each other in various ways. Close to the center of the Wheel, opposing spots easily complement each other. For example, Deep Meditation greatly prepares the Hunter's Mind. Both are a kind of meditative state, but one is very still and looks inward while the other is very active and looks outward. In contrast, further out toward the rim, opposing spots tend to clash strongly, even if they appear deceptively similar. For example, the Strong Ego clings to conscious self-control, while Disturbed Sleep brings dreams and nightmares that expose what the ego rejects. At the furthest extremes, Ecstatic Love is an intimate one-on-one connection and an alchemical antidote for Addiction, and activities that induce trance states (Hypnotherapy) are a great means to grow out of the Defiant Rebel.

The inner dotted circle around the Neutral Mind has arrows. This symbolizes the true nature of balance. Balance isn't static. Rather, like a tightrope walker, a person here is constantly rebalancing while moving because standing still or moving rigidly actually make the task difficult.

Finally, notice the labels along the outside of the Wheel, next to the arrows. The labels correspond to key aspects of the Jungian psyche, such as archetypes and ego. These labels indicate where the current epicenter of activity is in the psyche, where the person enjoys relatively high clarity. For example, persona and ego dominate in the Conflicting quadrant, while archetypes and chakras dominate in the Transforming quadrant. These are opportunities that result from time spent in the prior quadrant. One gets most in touch with one's true self after, say, passing through the Transforming gateway of *unio mystica*. These are aspects of the psyche that a person can focus on to work through and make the most of his or her time in that quadrant.

This is not a therapy handbook. If you want to delve deeply, consider a book or workshop by a kundalini yoga instructor or a Jungian depth psychologist like Dr. John Beebe.

In the coming pages, you will find symbolic views and longer descriptions of the four quadrants of the Wheel of Consciousness with suggestions to make the most of each one.

TRANSFORM

The little eye is you, as an observer. It is like the eye of a hurricane. All the little circles, squares, triangles, etc. are aspects of you and the world. Some aspects fit easily, while others don't. Every shape appears honestly as it is. Helpfully, the eye only sees what it can handle at that moment. The big dotted circle all around it represents the mystery and miracle of existence as well as your on-going healing process. The heart stands for a loving guide that appears to help your journey. Overall, your inner healer tends to get active and your chakras tend to be more sensitive to opening up.

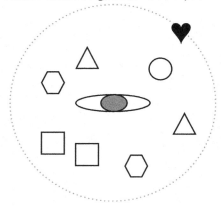

— Your psyche is fluid.
— Boundaries relax and are in flux.
— Issues appear clearly, as they really are, and are often personified in various ways, with less weight.
— An inner healing voice is active and your observer eye is open.
— Baggage tends to clear out.
— Chakras are relaxed and shifting.

SUFFER

At the center, your sense of self is fragmented, torn into pieces that overlap and compete. The big broken tilted box stands for an uncertain, unstable world. What is true or false? Who is helpful or harmful? The black dots indicate ongoing conflicts and issues. These include breaks within oneself. Each offers its own voice and views. Managing these is difficult. Mostly they push and pull you. There is no guide in the upper right corner, only emptiness and conflict that feels like existential angst or a "fake" god. Overall, your inner critic is hyperactive and chakra dysfunction invites danger.

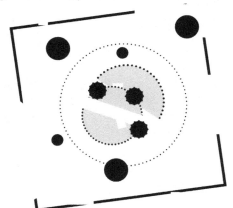

— Your psyche is fragmented.
— You may project a large, unstable, or false image of yourself.
— The world is confusing.
— Many issues and conflicts dog you.
— Lacking a trusted guide or anchor point.
— Aware that something is wrong but feel helpless to fix it.
— Caught in chakra whirlpool/s.

FLOW

The main circle is a "new" ego. It is renewed, whole, and harmonious. Its gray boundary means it is clear and flexible. The big box around it is dotted, indicating you know it is a map of the world—coherent, yet still with unknowns and areas to learn about. The little shapes represent conflicts to solve, needs to meet, and such. Their number is few, and you see more honestly what you need to work on. The bright sun provides light and energy to do that work. Overall, you are bright, patient, and still. You are less critical, with more open chakras, and also more discerning.

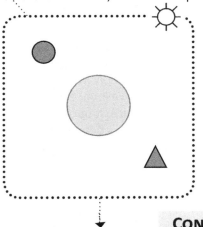

— Your psyche is peaceful.
— The world feels more open.
— Boundaries are clear and flexible.
— Your ego takes up less room.
— There are few issues, and they are
    less black-and-white and more gray.
— Life feels lighter.
— There's less baggage, more harmony.
— Chakras are healthier.

CONFLICT

The main circle is your ego—who you consciously think you are. It is solid, indicating strength and confidence. The big box around it is the world, as defined by your ego. The little dots are conflicts, unmet needs, pits of despair, and bad habits in your life. They stress you, and you mostly manage them. You may try to ignore them, project them onto others, occasionally suffer an outburst or anxiety, or have weird dreams. The gray star is a goal, idea or idol you cling to. It is your "Truth." Overall, your defenses and criticism of others tend to be active. Chakra flow is constricted and sluggish.

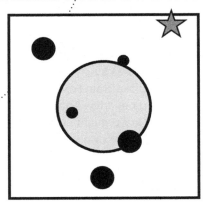

— Your psyche is rigid.
— The world feels known and closed.
— Your ego takes up a lot of room.
— Numerous issues dot your life.
— Life feels heavy.
— Your inner critic is strong and your
    inner observer eye is closed.
— Lots of baggage and sensitivities.
— Chakras are unbalanced.

TRANSFORM

This is the wheel's upper-left quadrant. Its metaphor is winter. In this space, we wander the proverbial land of the dead, whether it is a dream or a nightmare, and speak with the spirits of our ancestors and with little gods (archetypes). We face deep issues, let go of them, and receive wisdom.

We enter this space through the gateway of Deep Sleep. We let go of our plans and worries, addictions and distractions, and fall unconscious, surrendering ourselves to the unknown. This space is inherently psychological, reflecting the power of right-brain thinking. We explore, notice symbolism, explore meanings, reflect on ourselves, sort through our database of behaviors and life experiences, and engage in an open-ended journey into Shakespeare's "undiscovered country." The more we let go of our ego and accept going on a strange walk-about, the more we gain here.

In this quadrant, we may just daydream, oblivious to the outside world, or we may have vivid dreams and nightmares in actual Disturbed Sleep. We may be deeply Meditating, utilize Active Imagination, surrender to Hypnotherapy, or go on a shamanic Spirit Walk. All of these are passive and positive. They are opportunities to step outside everyday life and entrust ourselves to our unconscious. Even when the journey is frightening (such as battling a monstrous beast), or the activity itself is harsh (such as staying up all night), we make meaning and leave with a lesson or two. Working with chakras is a great way to engage this quadrant on a daily basis.

The rare closure to this quadrant is *Unio Mystica,* meaning boundless divine unity. Whatever the means, we get in touch with a universal Source and our true selves. The cycle then repeats.

SUFFER

This is the wheel's lower-left quadrant. Its metaphor is the fall season, when we relax to enjoy the fruit of our labors, or our labors have come to naught and we struggle halfheartedly to stay afloat. It is the space where we experience burnout, seek escape, and feel nostalgia for past glories.

We enter this space through the gateway of a Limbic Frenzy. We lost our grip, maybe due to exhaustion, defeat, or unresolved contradictions and tensions. Maybe we hit up against harsh practical obstacles, lived in denial of our own failings, fell into addiction, or neglected ourselves and loved-ones. Whatever the details, we played ourselves out. Psychologically, our shadow—rejected aspects of ourselves—plague us, and the downside of our complexes (Inferiority Complex, Savior Complex, etc.) dominate us, either quietly to their natural conclusion, or in disaster.

In this quadrant, we may engage in simple Passive Intake as a way to relax or we may get caught up in Addiction as a way to escape from life. We may suffer Brain Fog or a Depressing Loop, Hateful Self-Talk, or Memorializing. All of these are passive and negative. That is, we might get mindless, listening to music or watching television to decompress. Or we might suffer in the clutches of confusing, ugly feelings and a dull-witted consciousness as we binge or obsess. Words that describe this quadrant include *avoiding, clinging, escaping, longing, negating, numbing, obsessing,* and *wandering.*

Inevitably, we fall comatose, both literally and psychologically speaking. We surrender at this quadrant's exit, Deep Sleep, where we begin renewal and transformation.

FLOW

This is the wheel's upper-right quadrant. Its metaphor is the spring season, when warm sun shines again, rain falls, and foliage returns—growing and flowering with new life to eventually produce fruit. It is the space where we energize, learn, and innovate with our talents.

We may enter this space through the gateway of *Unio Mystica*, or boundless divine unity. We may experience this space in an obvious or subtle way, from a near-death experience to a moment of rapture while exploring nature. We also pass through this gate at birth, with our gifts and talents. Often, many small experiences slowly push us upward from adjacent quadrants. As adults, the more powerful the gateway experience, the more our true self is touched and our hidden, inner feminine side (*anima*) or masculine side (*animus*) is stimulated with creative potential. When our heroic self couples with our opposite, literally and/or psychologically, we blossom to perform at our best.

In this quadrant, we may experience Euphoric Bliss or Ecstatic Love. We may engage in Wise Facilitating, View Shifting, or Active Learning, or we flow in our Creative Zone. These are active and positive: gentle, beautiful, and clear-headed consciousness. We are generative here. We are using our talents to run with a new purpose or idea, and everything flows smoothly. We "live the dream." We create for the needs and benefit of everyone out of pure enjoyment. Words that describe this quadrant include *creativity, empathy, gratitude, helpfulness, innovation, intimacy, joy,* and *openness*.

Inevitably, as we encounter disruptions and obstacles, or as our burst of energy naturally wanes, we approach this quadrant's exit, Task Mode, where we will come into conflict with others.

CONFLICT

This is the wheel's lower-right quadrant. Its metaphor is summer, when whatever we planted in spring now thrives, growing strong and tall with slowly ripening fruit. It is the space where we produce *en masse*, separate good from bad fruit, and achieve success.

We enter this space through the gateway of the Task Mode. Society tends to encourage this mode. It is inherently practical, reflecting the power of left-brain thinking. It is highly "goal-focused." We use it to set goals, make plans, explain, decide, correct, and overall work from values and principles. The clearer we get on who we are, what we do, how and why, the easier this quadrant will be as we deal with its many challenges. Success here requires a strong, healthy ego as a homebase (or castle) and an effective persona. Our persona is the face we present to the world.

In this quadrant, we rely on our Hunter's Mind or a Strong Ego. Or we do Ego-Enhancing, start Manipulating others, teeter in a Hypersensitive state, or react with Rebel Defiance. These are active and negative. We are in a state of conflict, a tug-of-war with others, whether sneaky or aggressive. Our foe can be real or imagined. This conflict is inevitable, though it does not harm us yet. It helps us to get things done, or at least avoid being done in, as our aims collide with others. Words that describe this quadrant include *building, capturing, defending, maneuvering, promoting, pushing, resisting,* and *tracking*.

We inevitably suffer a defeat, run out of resources, or trip on our inner demons. We "lose it" at this quadrant's exit, a Limbic Frenzy, which takes us into avoidance, negativity, and suffering.

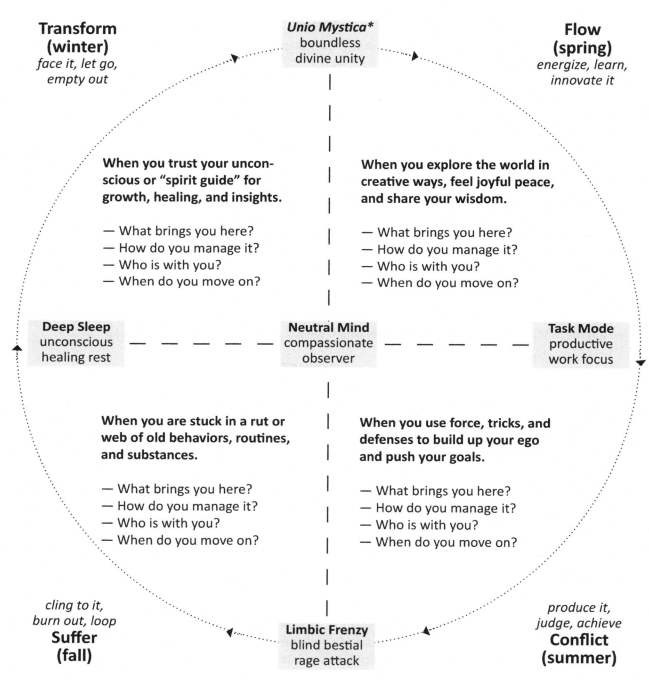

**Transform
(winter)**
*face it, let go,
empty out*

Unio Mystica*
boundless
divine unity

**Flow
(spring)**
*energize, learn,
innovate it*

When you trust your unconscious or "spirit guide" for growth, healing, and insights.

— What brings you here?
— How do you manage it?
— Who is with you?
— When do you move on?

When you explore the world in creative ways, feel joyful peace, and share your wisdom.

— What brings you here?
— How do you manage it?
— Who is with you?
— When do you move on?

Deep Sleep
unconscious
healing rest

Neutral Mind
compassionate
observer

Task Mode
productive
work focus

When you are stuck in a rut or web of old behaviors, routines, and substances.

— What brings you here?
— How do you manage it?
— Who is with you?
— When do you move on?

When you use force, tricks, and defenses to build up your ego and push your goals.

— What brings you here?
— How do you manage it?
— Who is with you?
— When do you move on?

*cling to it,
burn out, loop*
**Suffer
(fall)**

Limbic Frenzy
blind bestial
rage attack

*produce it,
judge, achieve*
**Conflict
(summer)**

Figure 7: Respond to the prompts to explore the Wheel for yourself

Chakra Art Therapy

Drawing is a great way to explore the chakras. You can focus on one chakra, represent your experience of the whole chakra system, or aim for some other intention.

No artistic talent is required. Simple free-form sketching is fine, as is a collage of Internet clip art. Feel free to start with a prompt such as an animal, geometric shape, or everyday object; then allow your unconscious to guide your hand to expand on that prompt. This is more relaxing and revealing than striving to implement a specific idea, which tends to bring in our ego and critical inner voice. You are welcome to print and use the frame below to create a chakra tableau. However you draw, you will likely gain some insight into your psyche.

Here are some suggestions to draw tableaus. For each chakra, focus on key characteristics. For example, where is the ego and what does it look like? A circle in the center is a start. Then add to it. Also, what element predominates? Select from earth, water, fire, wood, air, metal, void or light. Where is the image more dark or light? Next, select symbols. You might read about the chakra and select symbols that come to mind as you read. Symbols may be simple. Give extra consideration to how your symbols work together and thus where they sit on the page. For example, masculine and feminine symbols might be adjacent or opposing. Overall, strive for balance and trust your gut feel as you draw. If needed, let your hand draw where it may and then decide on the meaning.

About the Author

Dario Nardi, Ph.D. is a world-renowned author, speaker, and expert in the fields of neuroscience and personality. He holds a position of senior lecturer at University of California (Los Angeles), where he won UCLA's Copenhaver Award for Innovative Use of Technology in 2005 and UCLA's Distinguished Teacher of the Year in 2011. At UCLA, he has taught in Anthropology and Program in Computing as well as the university's Honors Collegium.

Dario is the owner of Radiance House, which publishes workbooks, manuals, software, and other aids for use by Human Resources consultants and trainers for major organizations in the USA and around the world. Visit the online store at www.RadianceHouse.com.

Dario's books include *Neuroscience of Personality*, *Our Brains in Color*, and *8 Keys to Self-Leadership*, among other titles. He is the creator of the Personality Types and Love Therapy apps for the iPhone. He was certified in psychological testing in 1994 and gained further training as an Interstrength Associate under organizational psychologist and systems thinker Linda Berens, PhD.

Dario is also an author of adventure games and game fiction.

Since 2007, Dario has focused his time on conducting hands-on brain research utilizing insights from real-time EEG technology. He regularly keynotes at conferences and facilitates workshops teaching professionals in multiple countries the art and science of the brain.

Dario began study of kundalini yoga and entheogens in 2014. He conducts brain imaging pilot research on altered states of consciousness and is a professional provider in the InnerSpace Integration Support Network found at www.innerspaceintegration.com.

You can learn more at www.DarioNardi.com, www.Facebook.com/NeuroTypes, and www.Facebook.com/JungOnYoga.

References

Bhajan, Yogi. *The Chakras: Kundalini Yoga as Taught by Yogi Bhajan*. Kundalini Research Institute, 2013.

Berens, Linda and Nardi, Dario. *Understanding Yourself and Others: An Introduction to the Personality Type Code*. Radiance House, 2004.

Bucke, Richard M. *Cosmic Consciousness: A Study in the Evolution of the Human Mind*. Merchant Books, 2015.

Geyer, Peter. "Jung's Letters: A Perusal and Commentary". Presented at the International Association of Psychological Type Biennial Conference, 2017.

Geyer, Peter. "Type, Self and Personality". Presented at the Ninth Australian National Association of Psychological Type Conference, 2010.

Heaven, Ross. *The Hummingbird's Journey to God: Perspectives on San Pedro, the Cactus of Vision*. O Books, 2009.

Henshaw, John. "Carl Jung and the Kundalini". *Knowledge of Reality*, Issue 12-2, 2006. [Website]. Retrieved from http://www.sol.com.au/kor/12_02.htm

Jung, C. G. with Sonu Shamdasani (editor) et. al. *The Red Book: A Reader's Edition*. W. W. Norton & Company, 2012.

Jung, C. G. *Psychological Types: The Collected Works of C.G. Jung Volume 6*. Princeton University Press, 1976.

Jung, C. G. *Two Essays on Analytical Psychology: The Collected Works of C.G. Jung Volume 7*. Princeton University Press, 1972.

Kilham, Chris. *The Ayahuasca Test Pilot's Handbook*. Evolver Editions, 2014.

Myers, Isabel Briggs. *Gifts Differing*. Consulting Psychologists Press, 1980.

Myers, Steve. "The Five Functions of Psychological Type". *Journal of Analytical Psychology*, Volume 61, Issue 2, pages 183–202, April 2016.

Nardi, Dario. *8 Keys to Self-Leadership: From Awareness to Action*. Radiance House, 2005.

Nardi, Dario. *Your Brain in Altered States.* [PDF PowerPoint document]. Retrieved from http://www.Facebook.com/NeuroTypes/

Nummenmass, Lauri et al. *Bodily Maps of Emotions.* Proceedings of the National Academy of Sciences, 2014.

Ouspensky, P.D. *The Fourth Way: A lucid explanation of the practical side of G.I. Gurdjieff's teachings.* Knoph, 1957.

Oroc, James. *Tryptamine Palace: 5-MeO-DMT and the Sonoran Desert Toad.* Park Street Press, 2009.

Power, Laura. *The 8 Biotypes.* [Website]. Retrieved from http://www.biotype.net/types/

Rattana, Guru. *Introduction to Kundalini Yoga and Meditation: Volume 1 – Begin and Deepen Your Practice.* Yoga Technology LLC, 2015.

Ravalec, Vincent, et al. *Iboga: The Visionary Root of African Shamanism.* Park Street Press, 2007.

Shamdasani, Sonu, Editor. *C.G. Jung: The Psychology of Kundalini Yoga.* Princeton University Press, 1996.

van der Kolk, Bessel. *The Body Keeps the Score: Brain, Mind, and Body in the Healing of Trauma.* Penguin Books, 2015.

Wallis, Christopher. *The Six Most Important Things You Never Knew About the Chakras.* [Website]. Retrieved from http://www.tantrikstudies.org/blog/2016/2/5/the-real-story-on-the-chakras

Wallis, Christopher. *Why Spiritual Growth Does Not Lead to Enlightenment.* [Website]. Retrieved from http://www.tantrikstudies.org/blog/2016/3/3/why-spiritual-growth-does-not-lead-to-enlightenment

Please visit www.RadianceHouse.com for resources!

Made in the USA
Middletown, DE
06 April 2019